COMMON GROUND

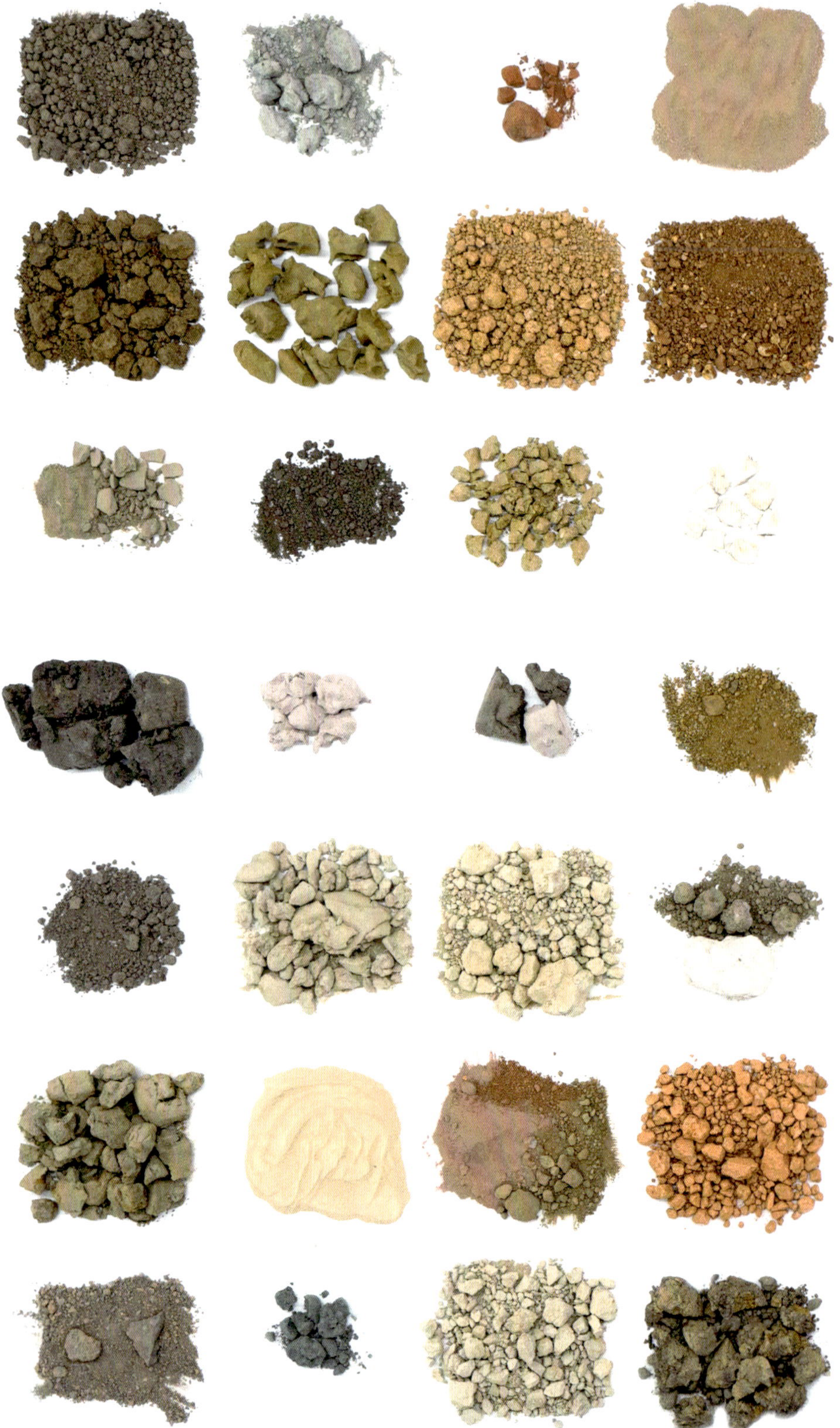

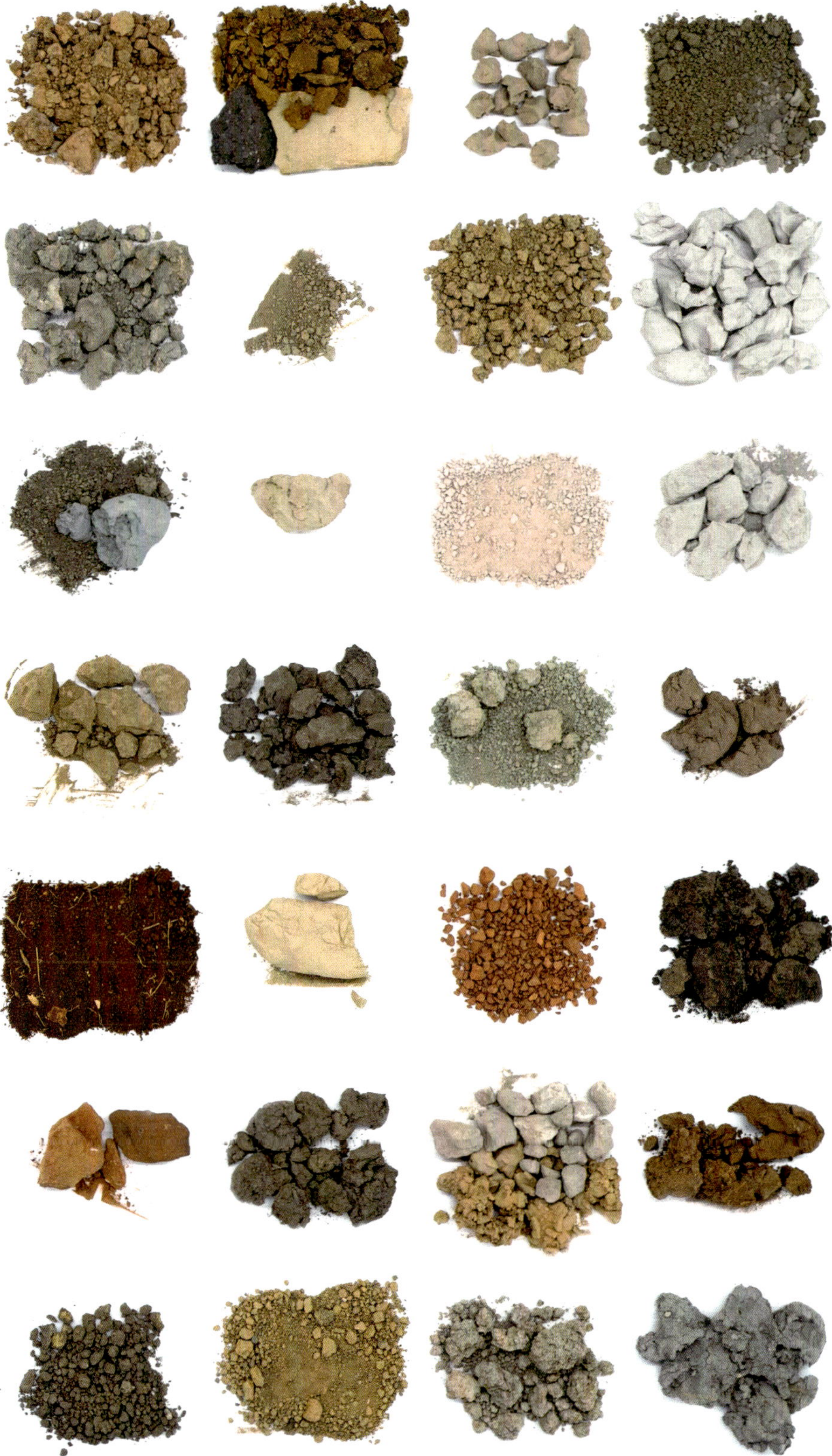

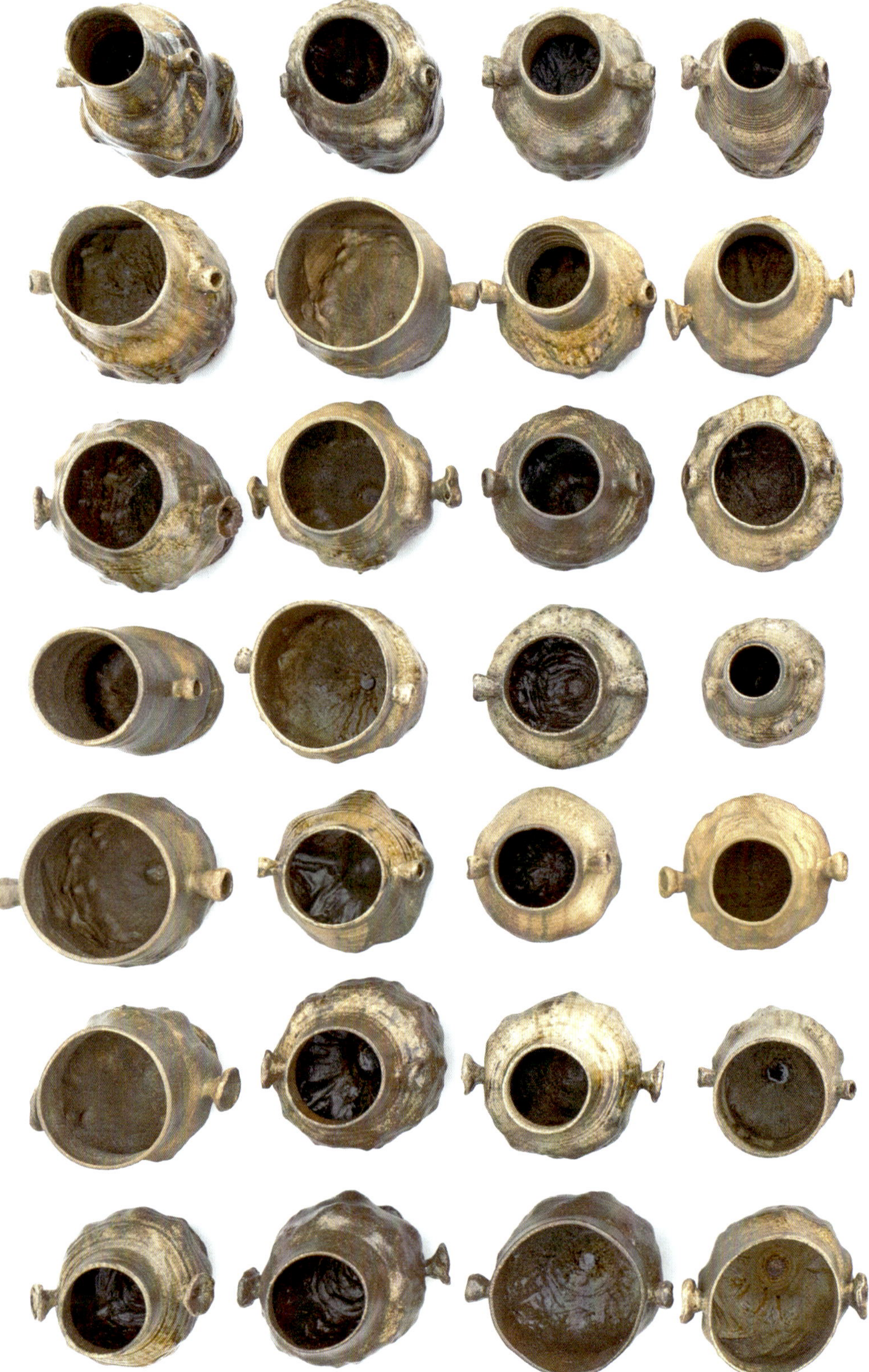

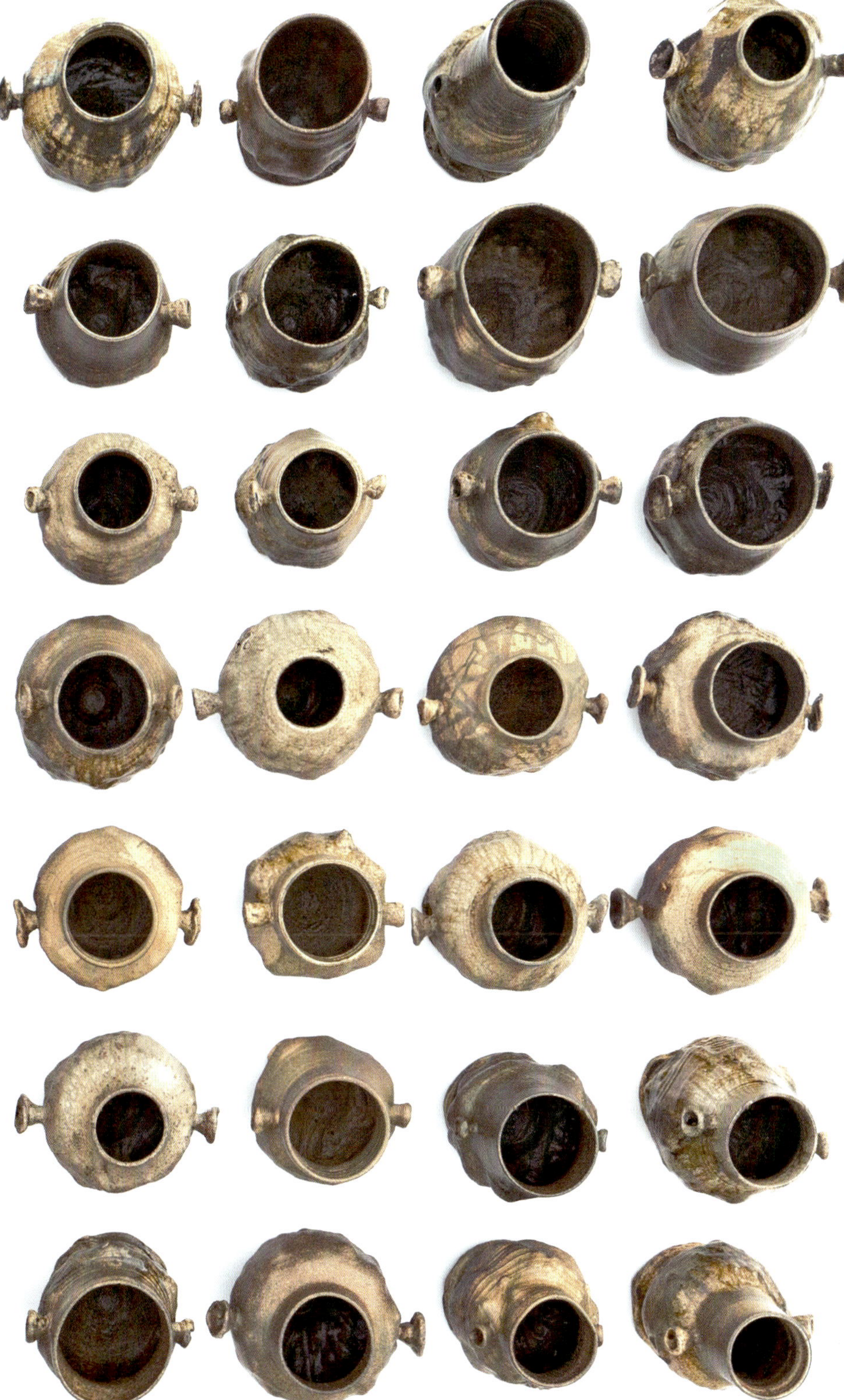

COMMON GROUND

ADAM SILVERMAN
+
SOGETSU IKEBANA LOS ANGELES

INVENTORY PRESS

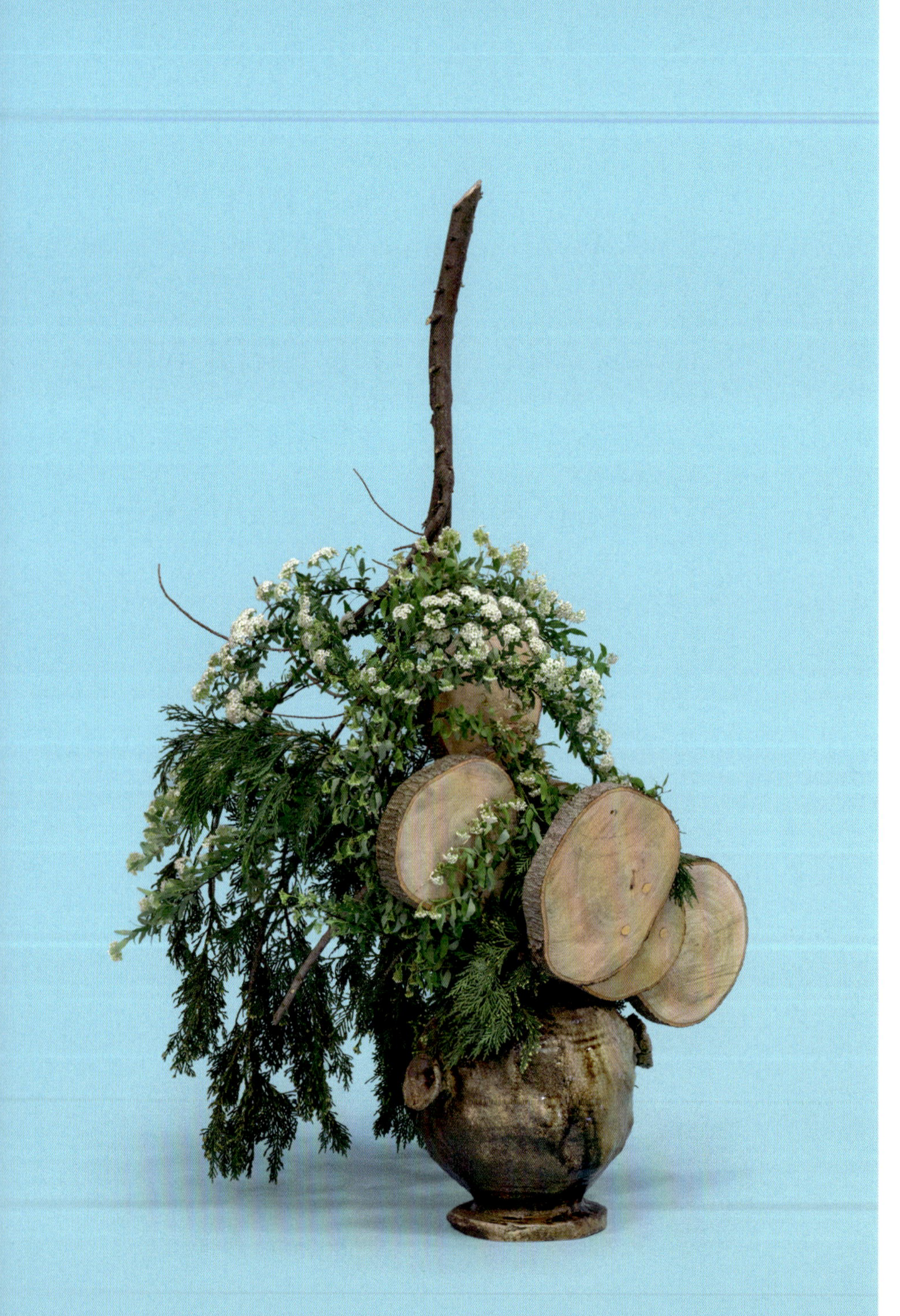

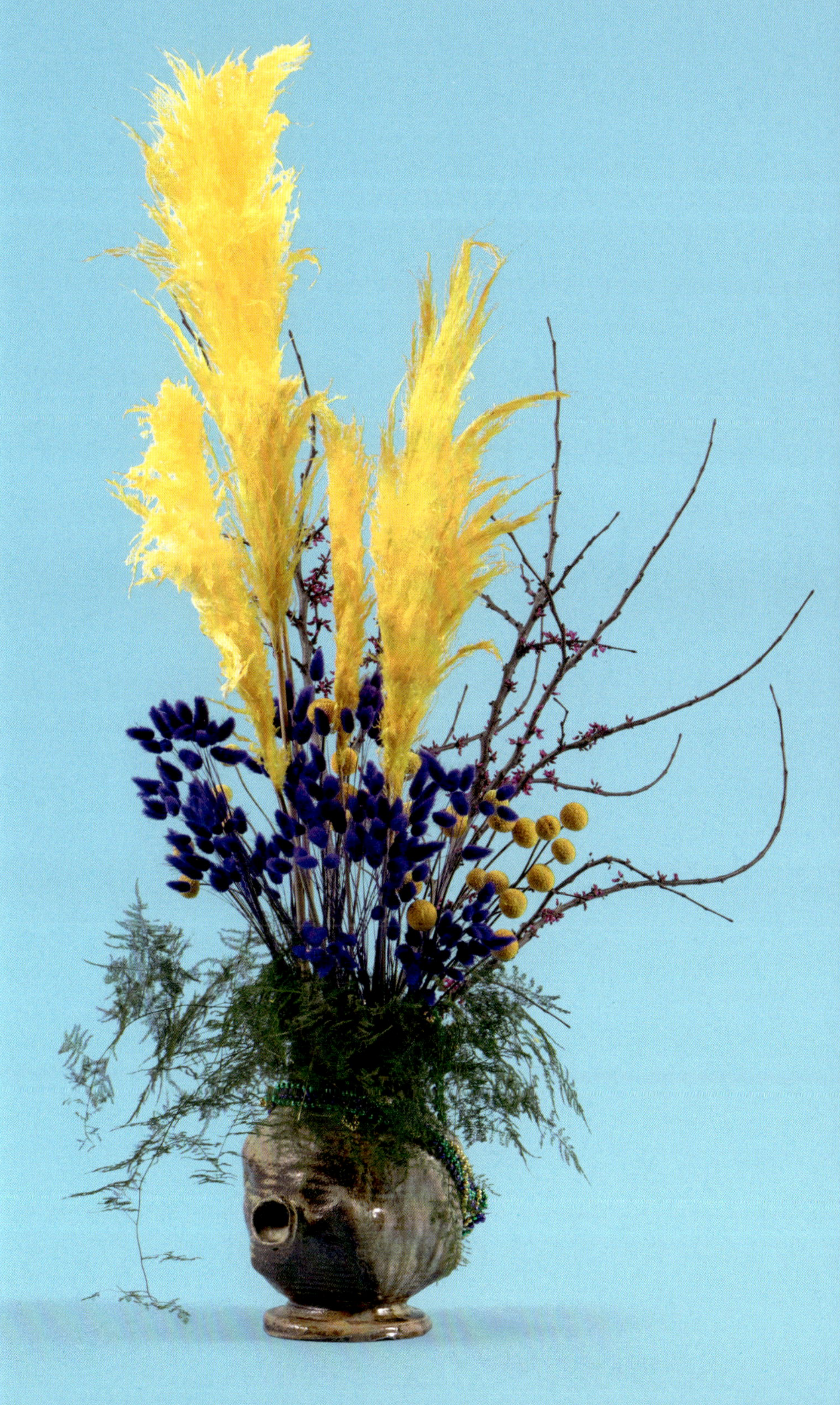

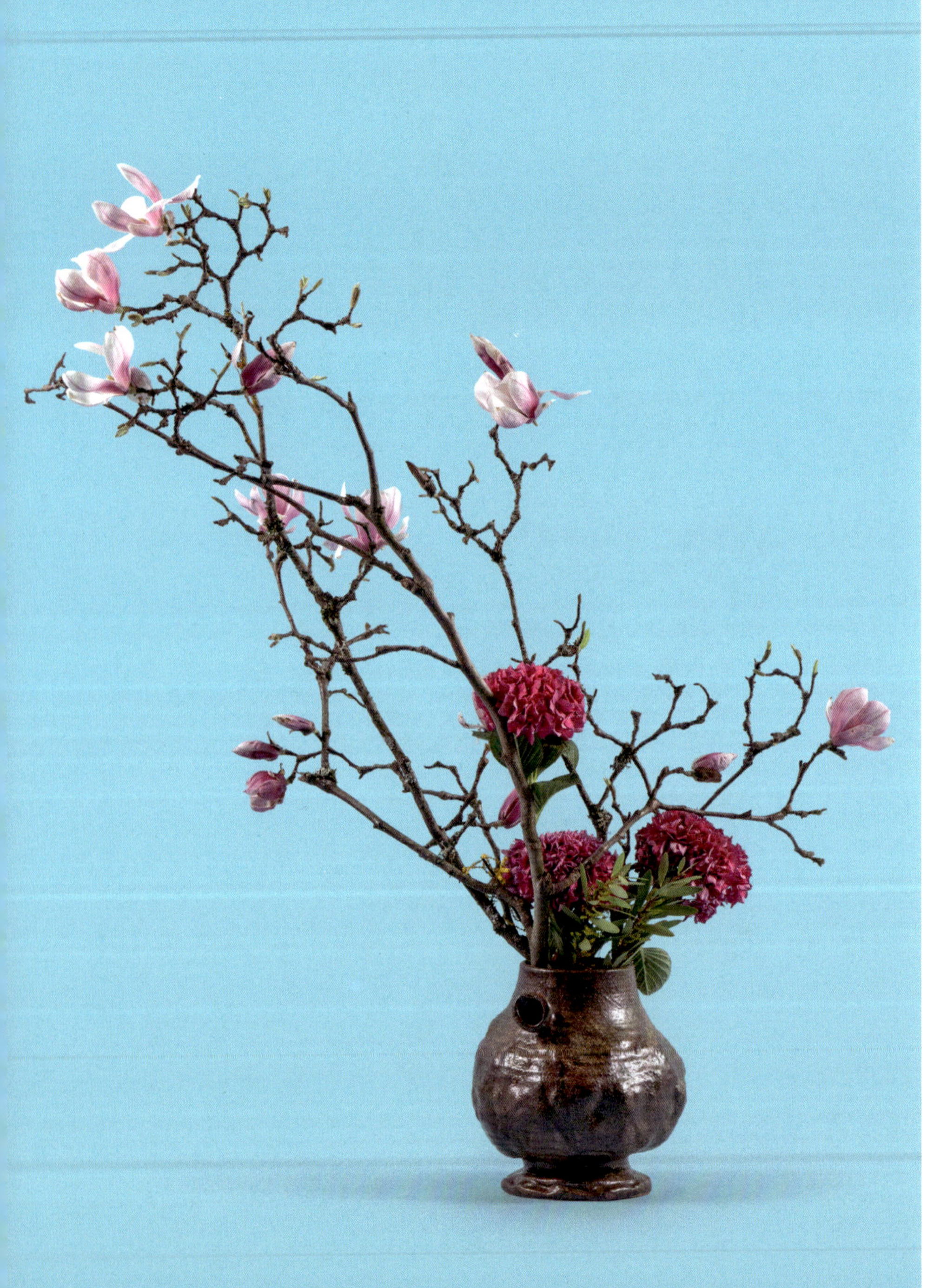

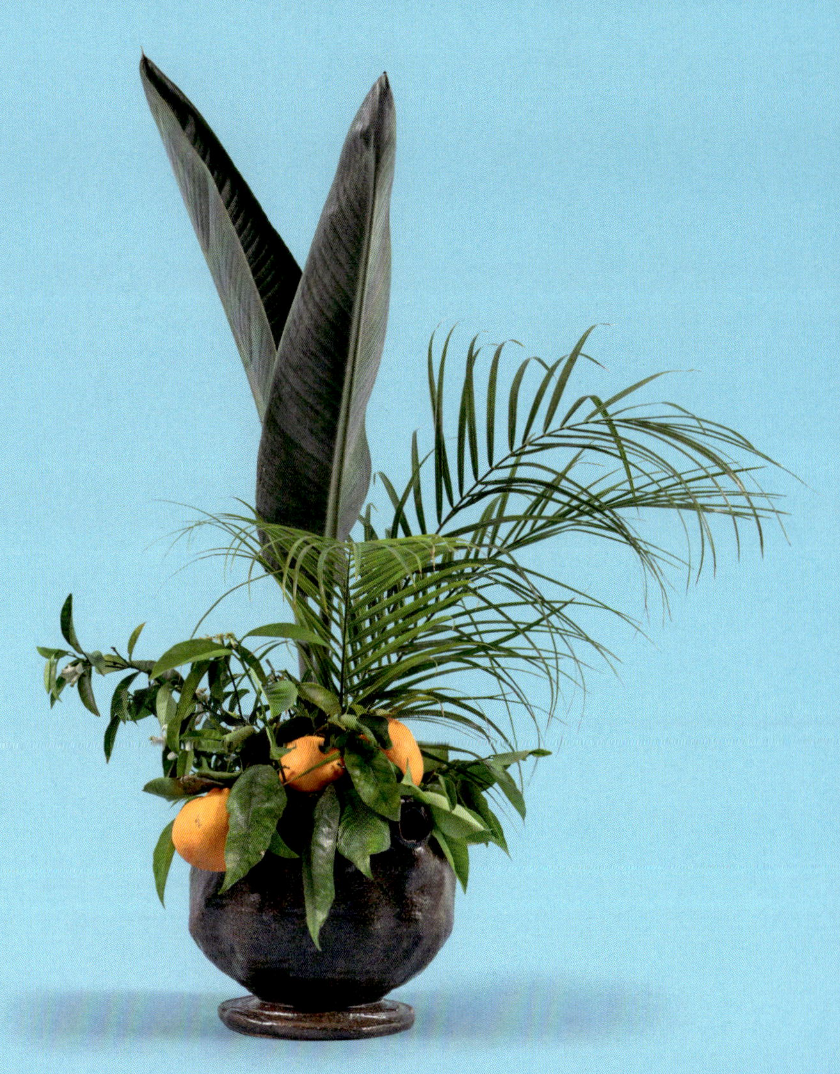

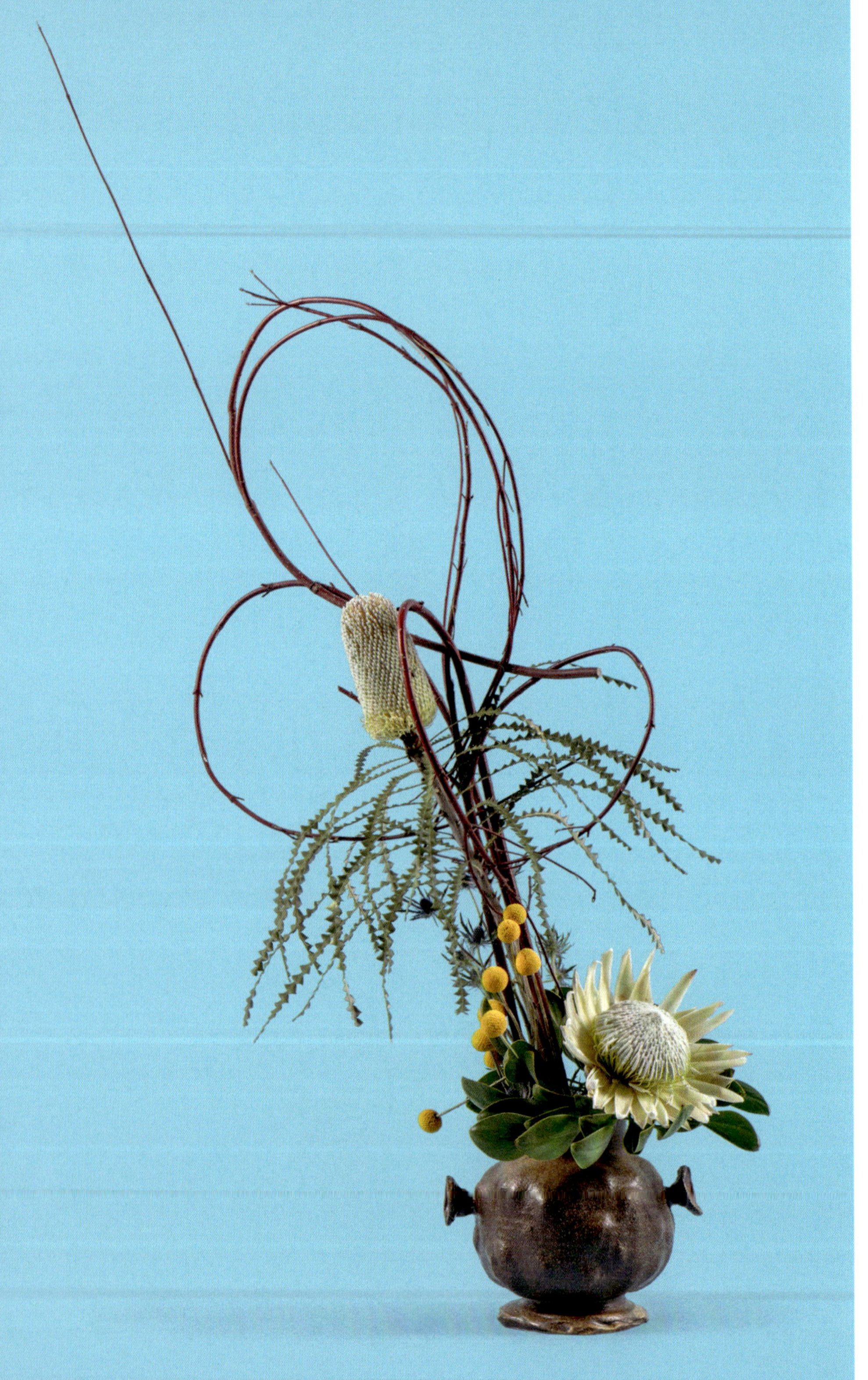

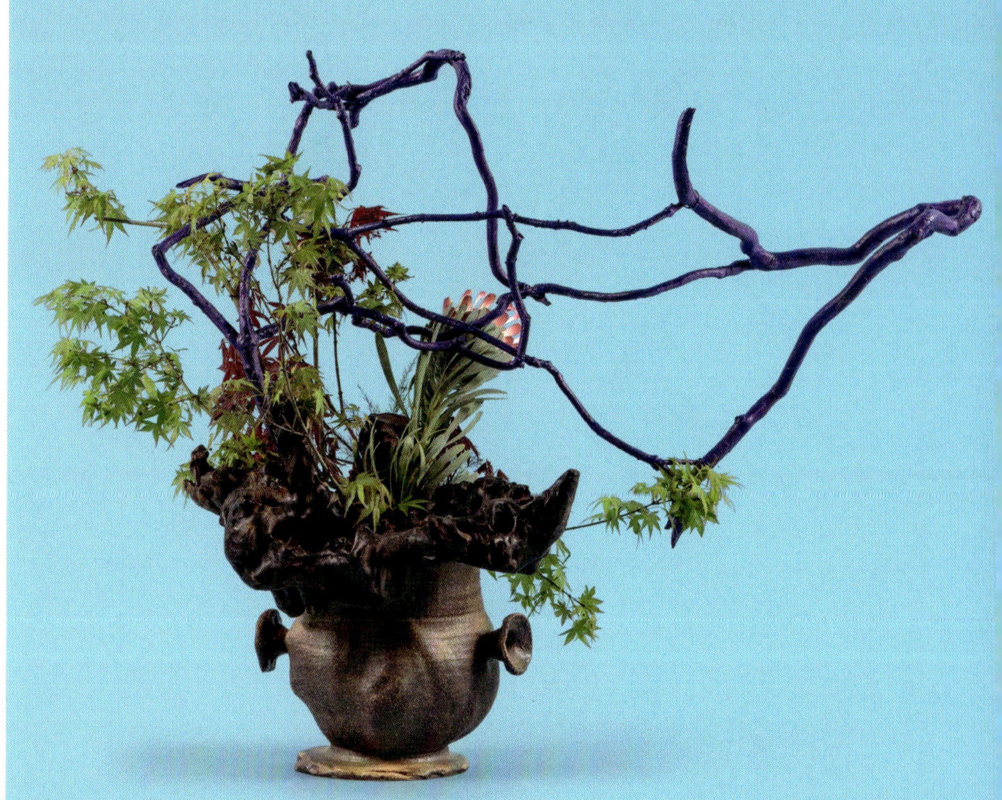

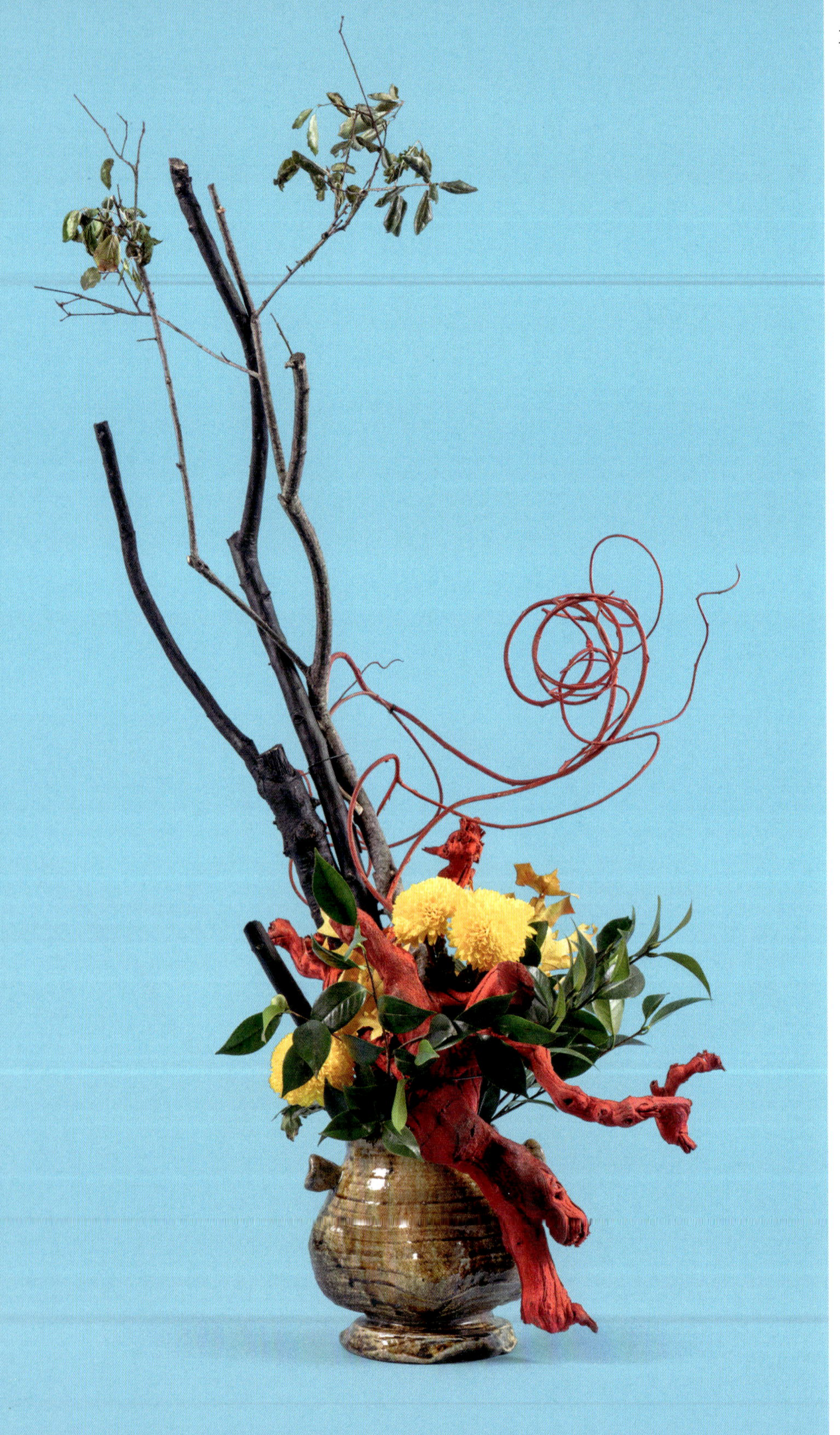

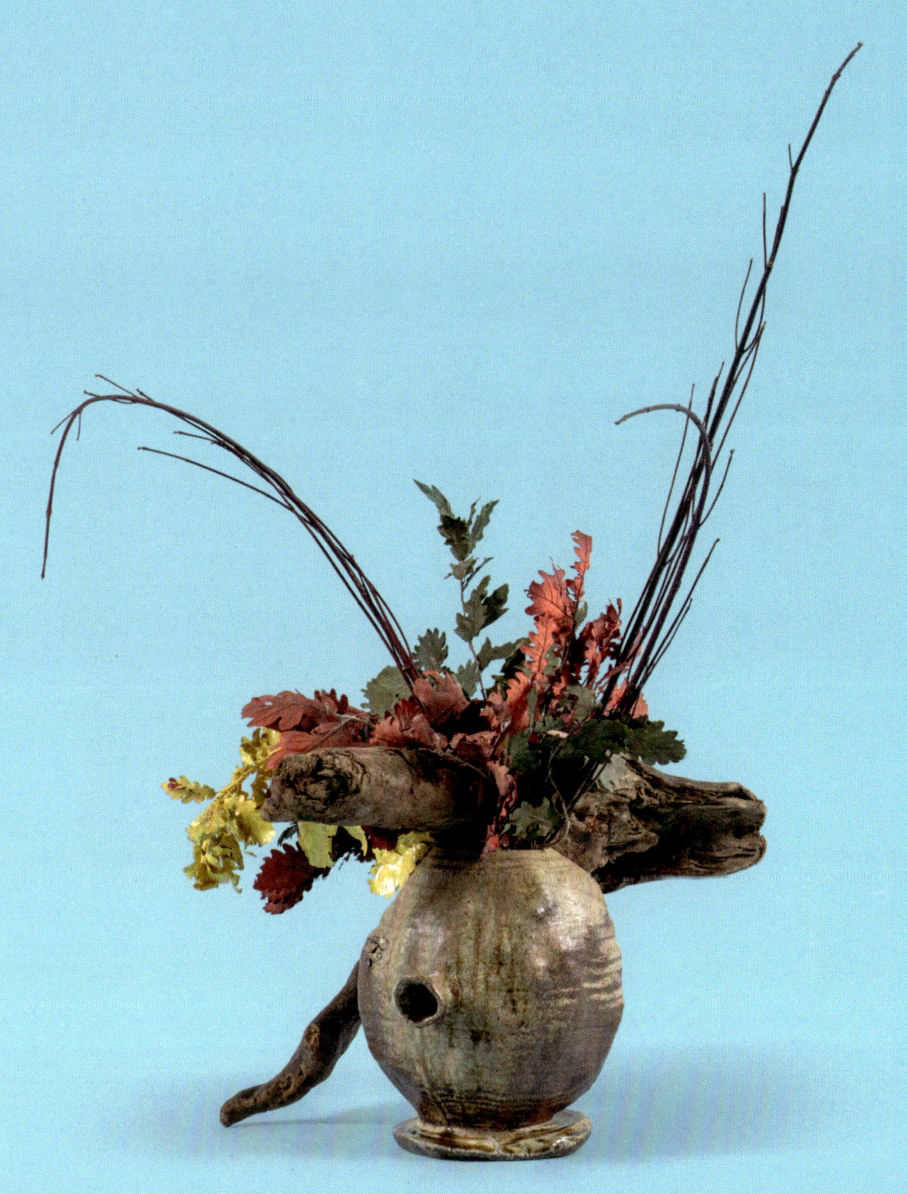

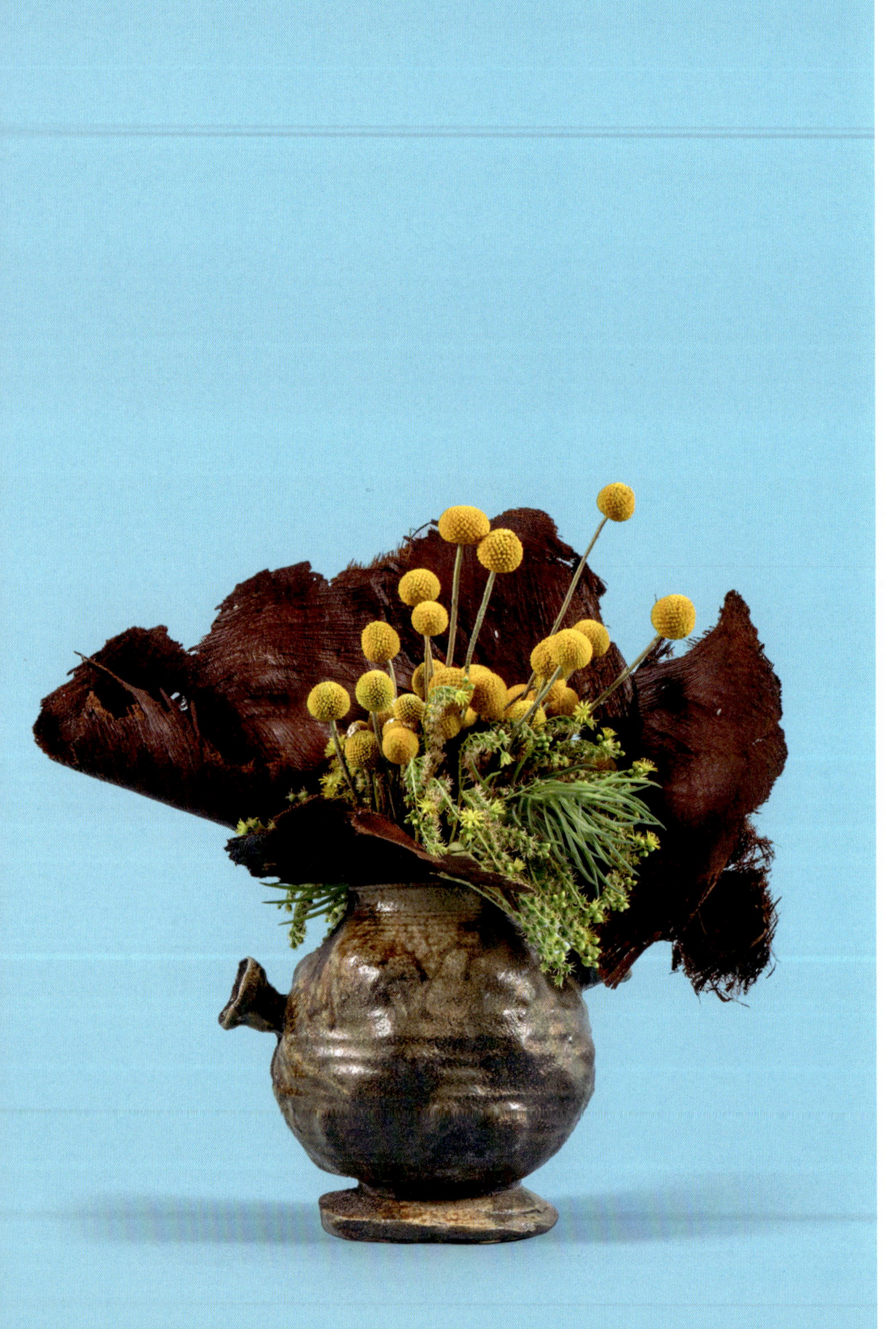

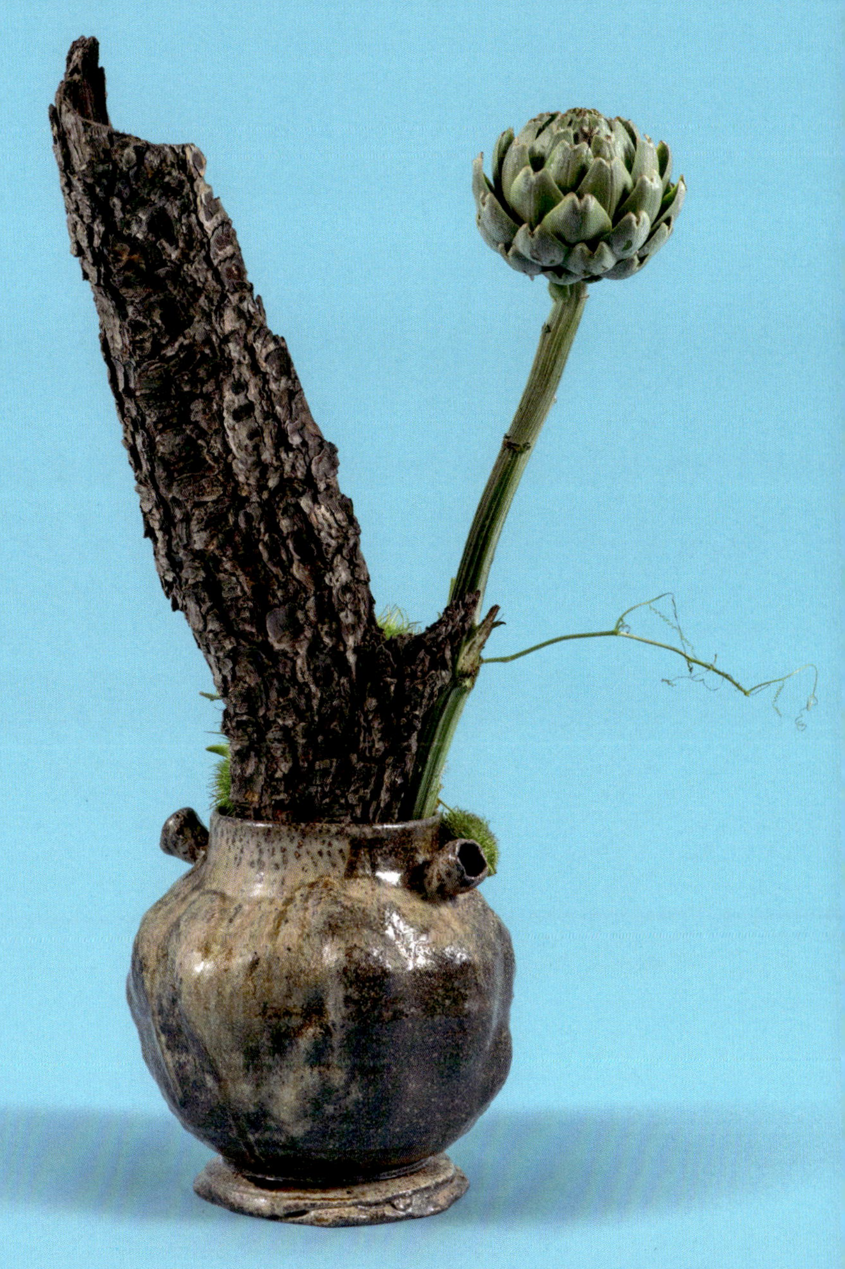

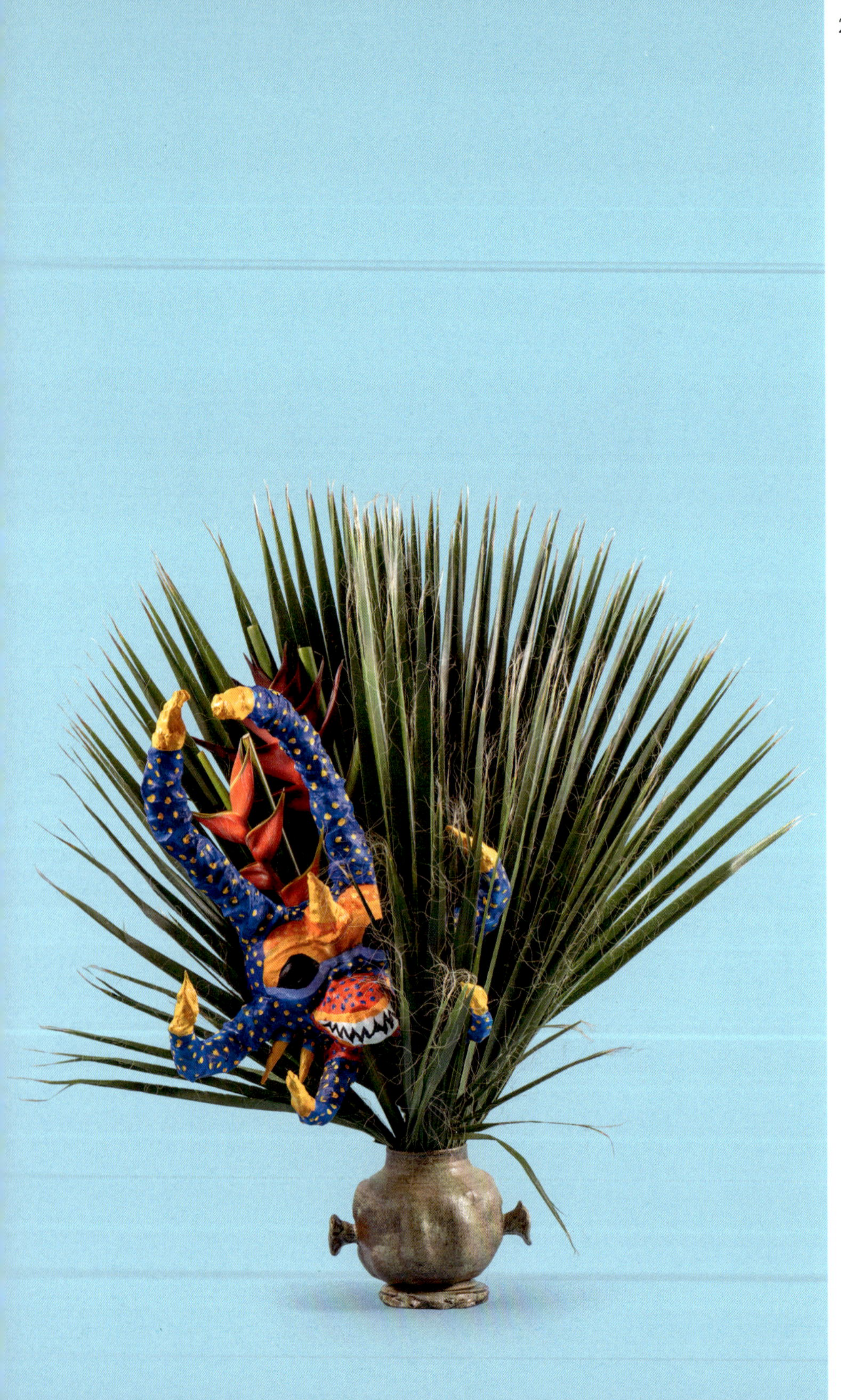

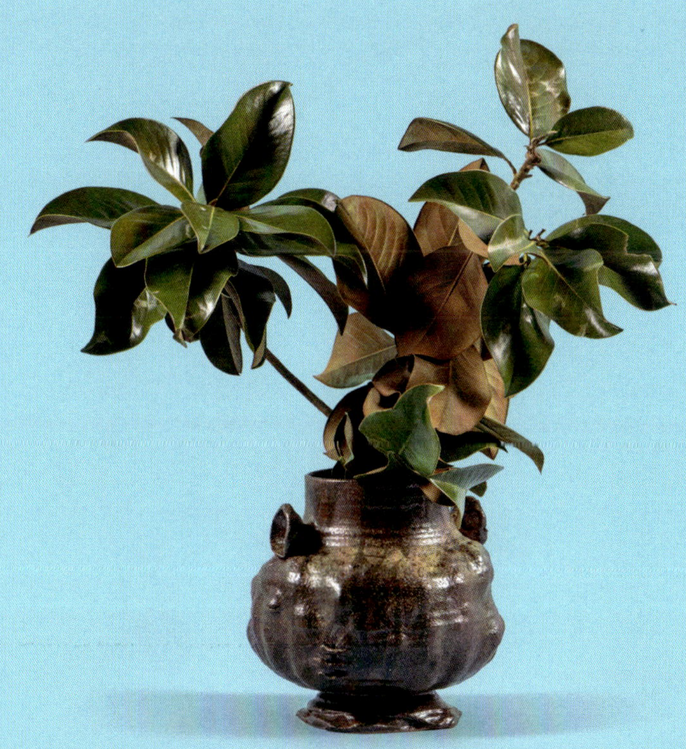

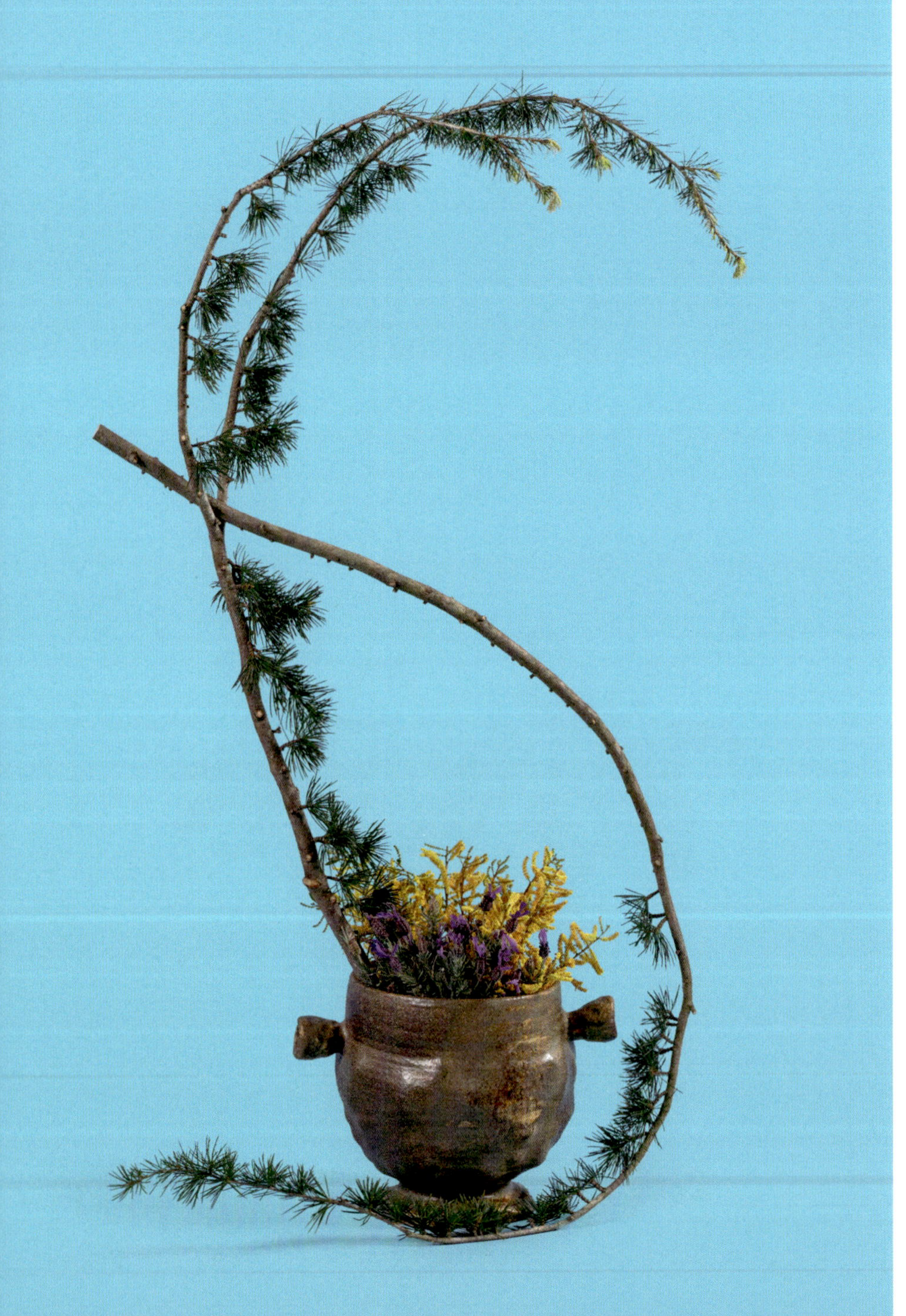

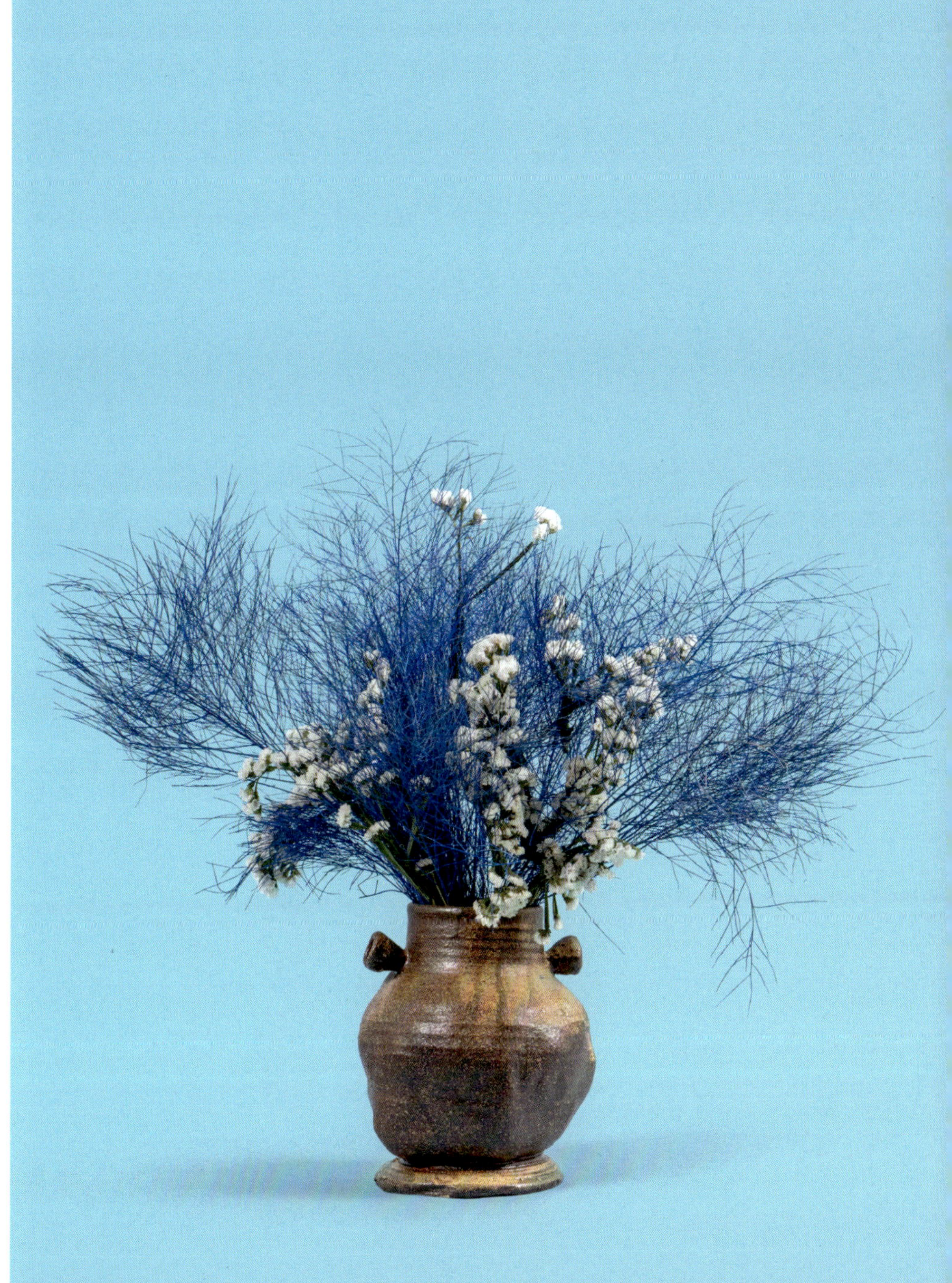

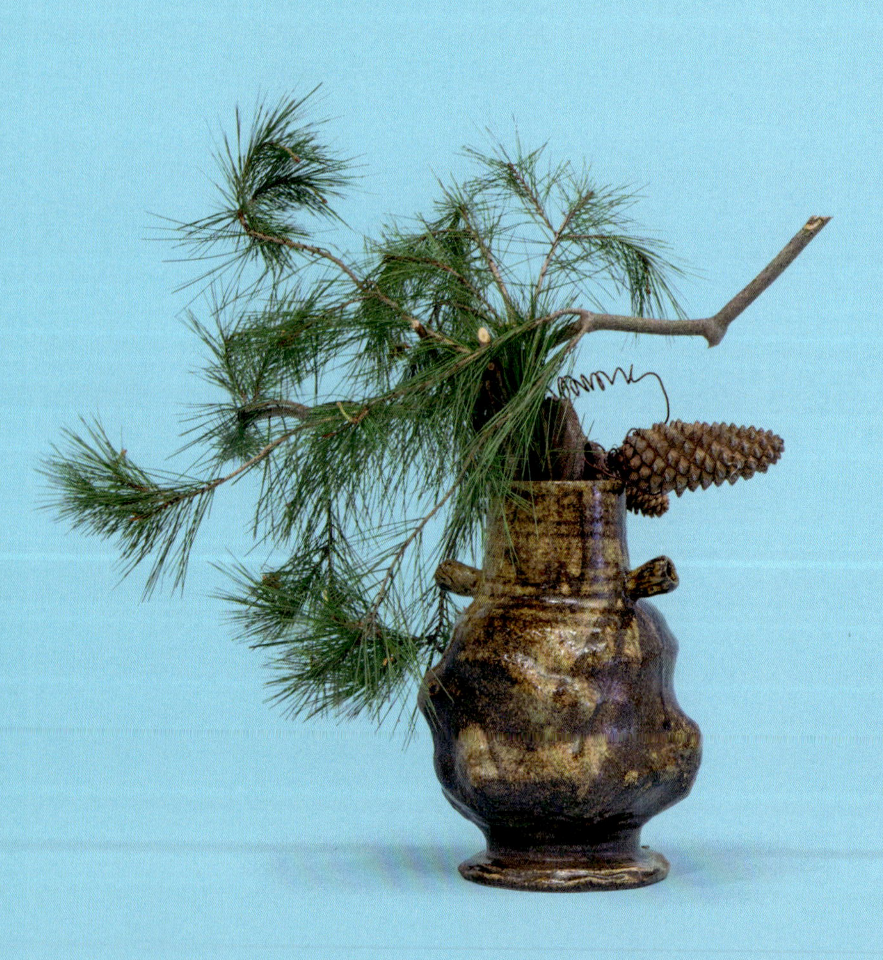

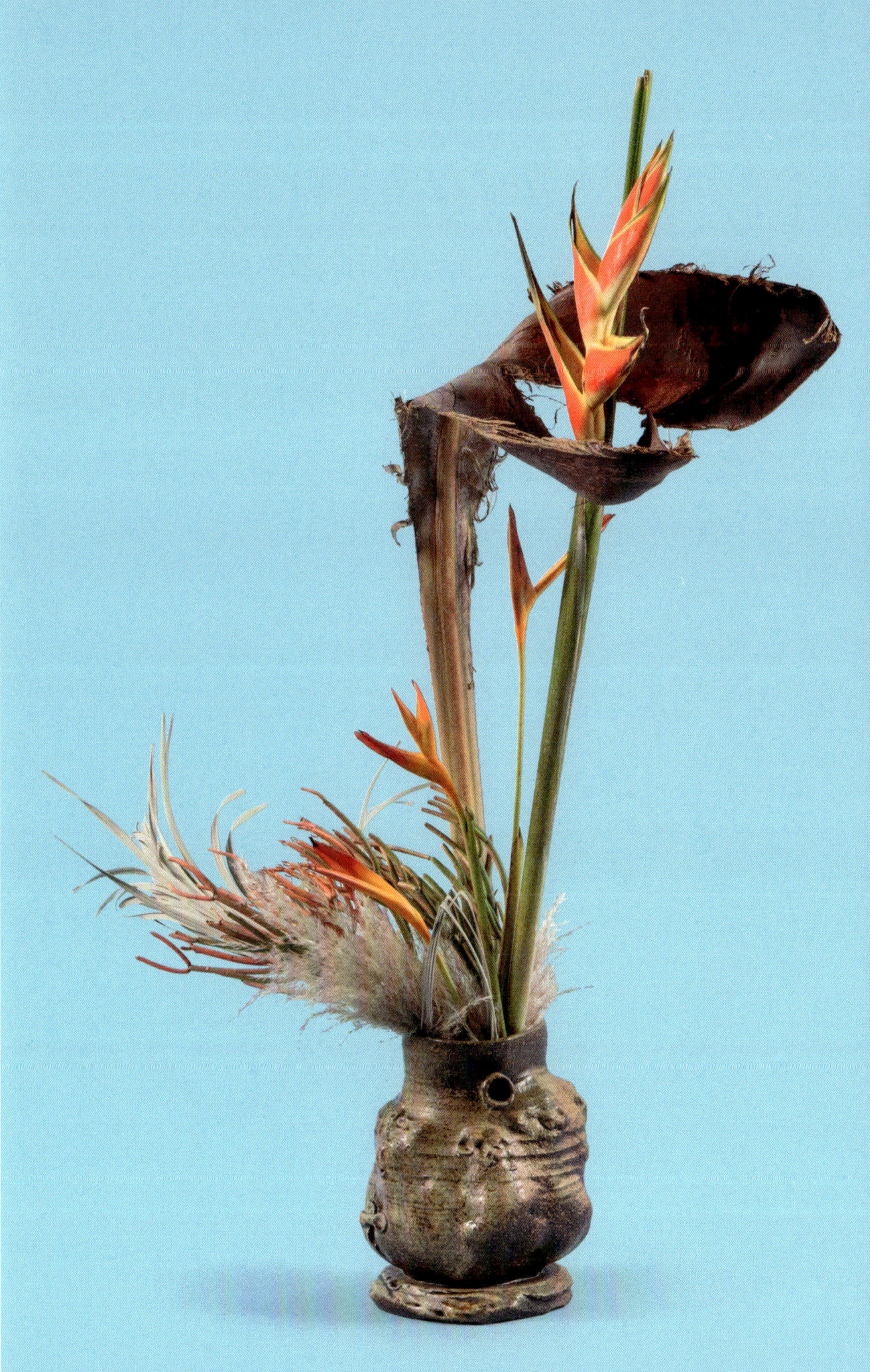

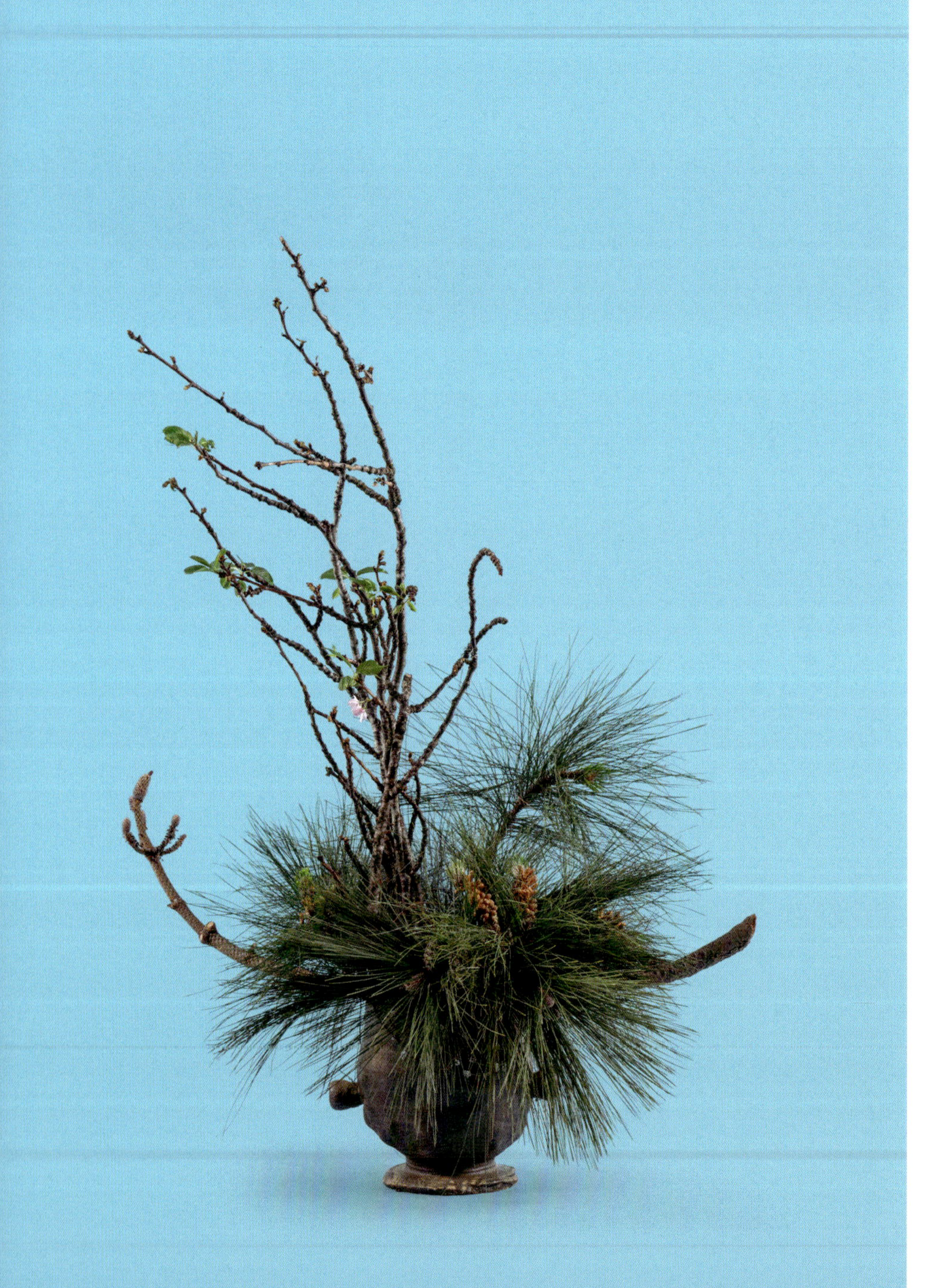

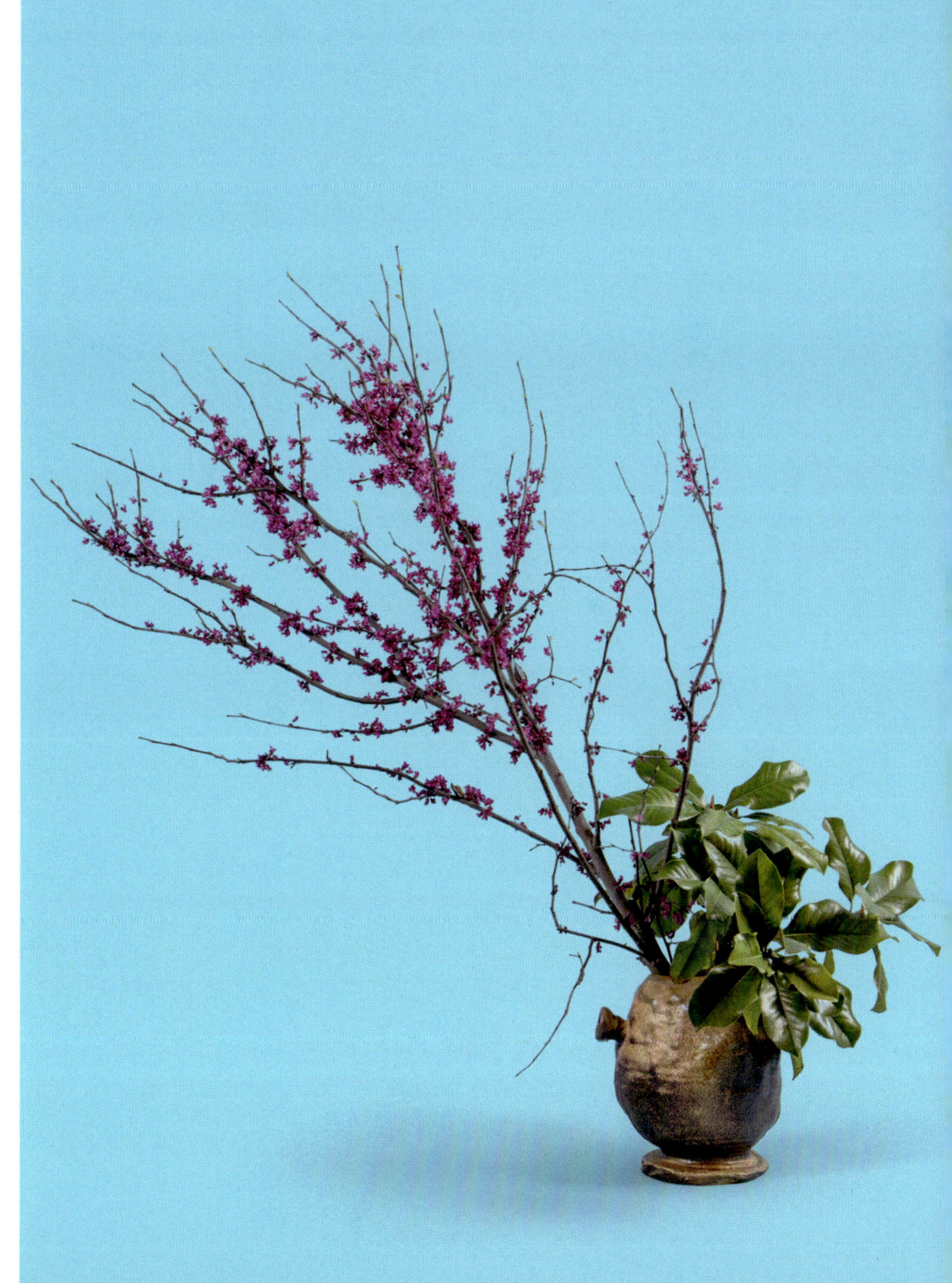

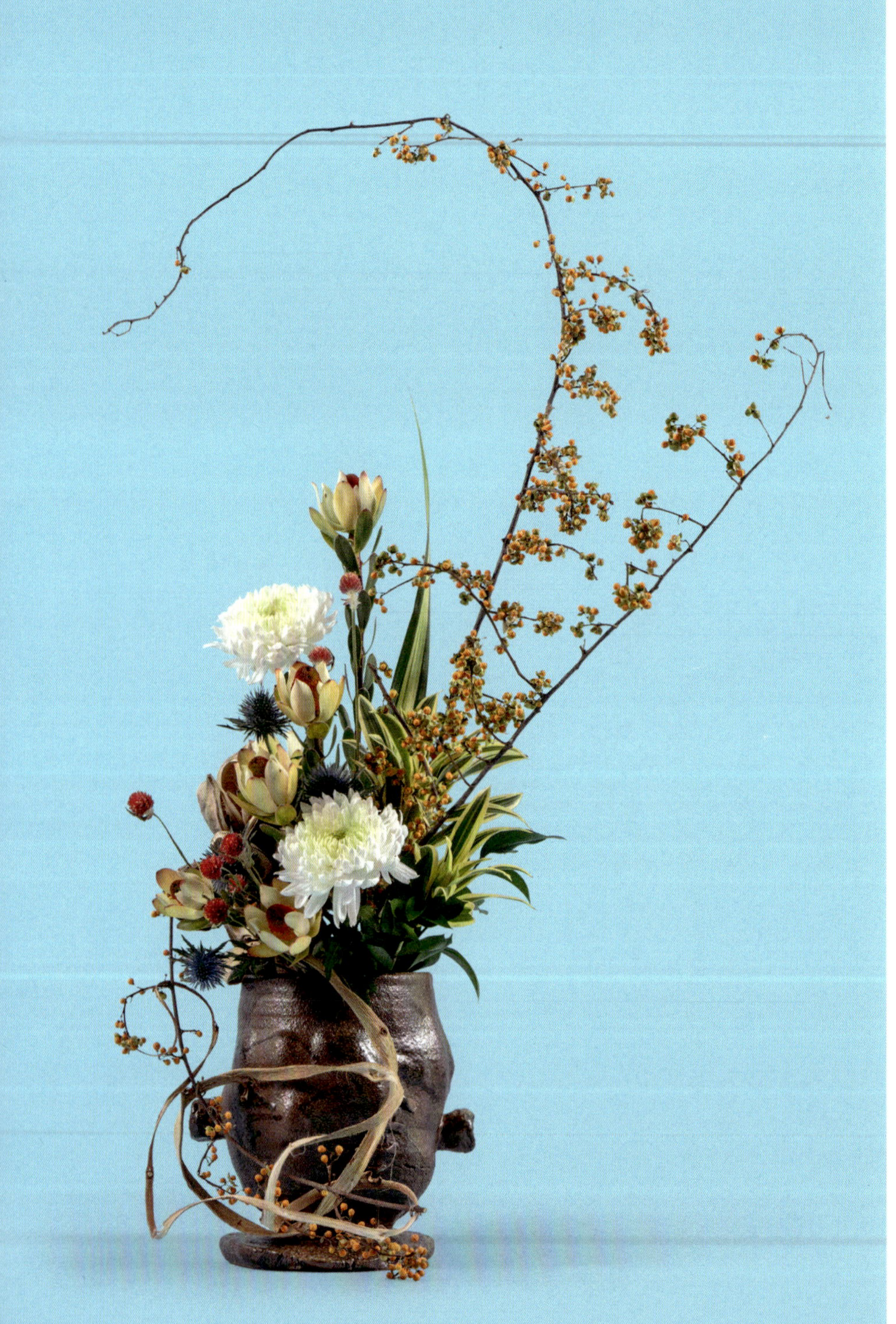

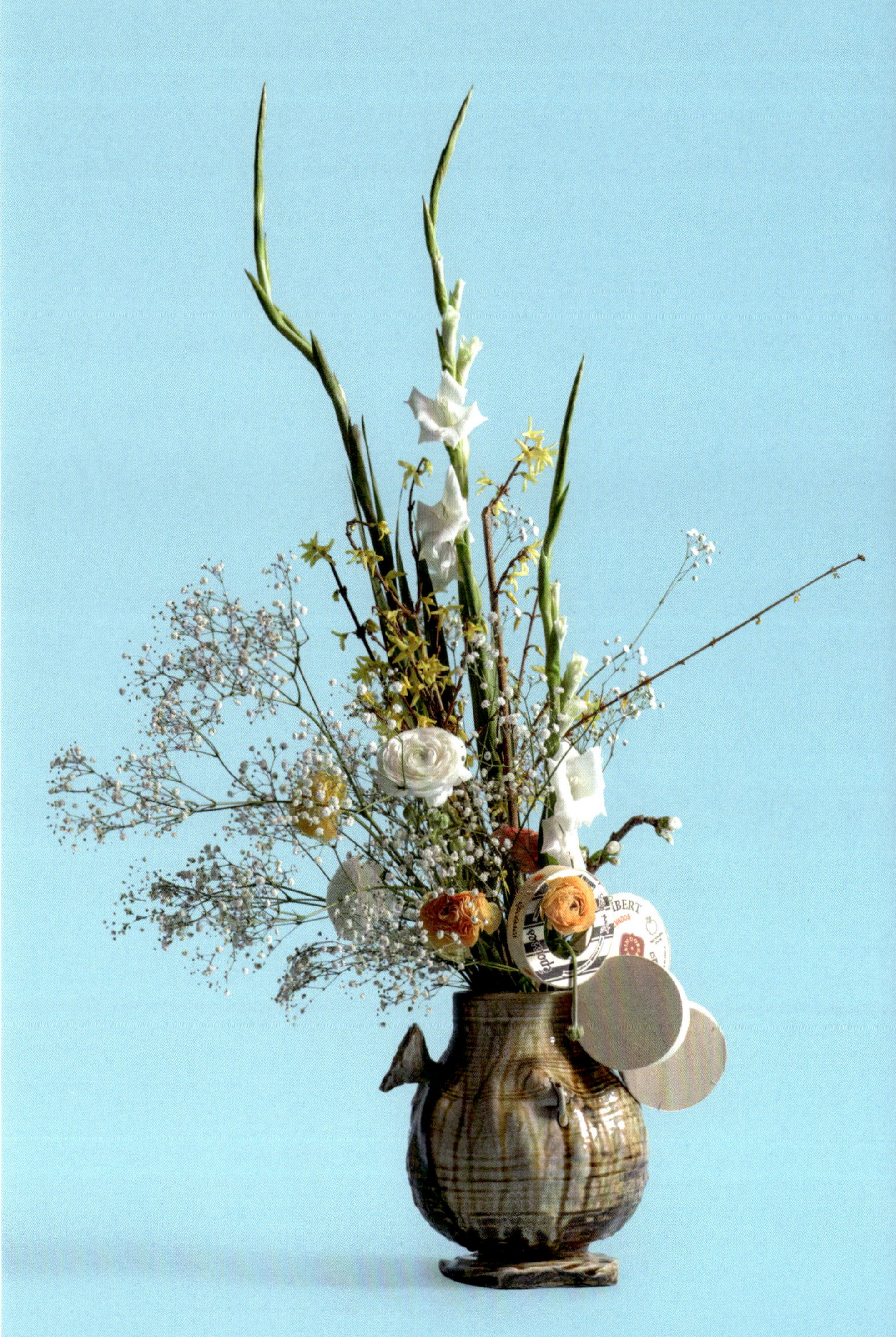

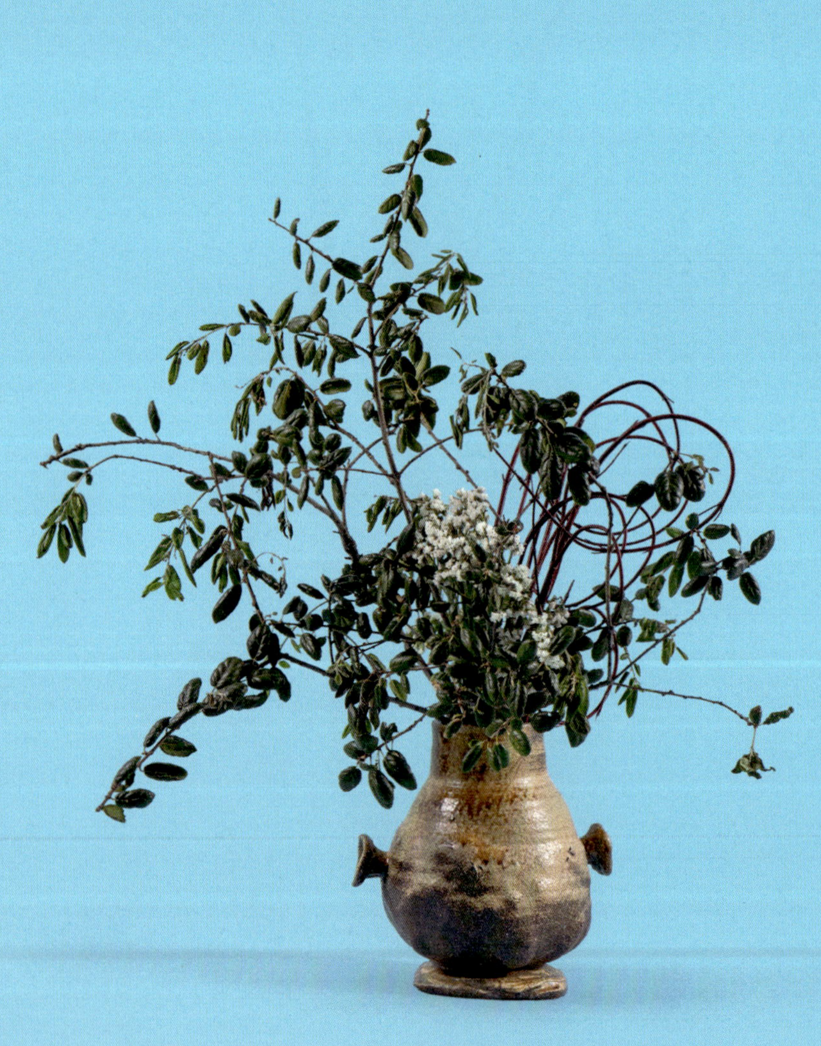

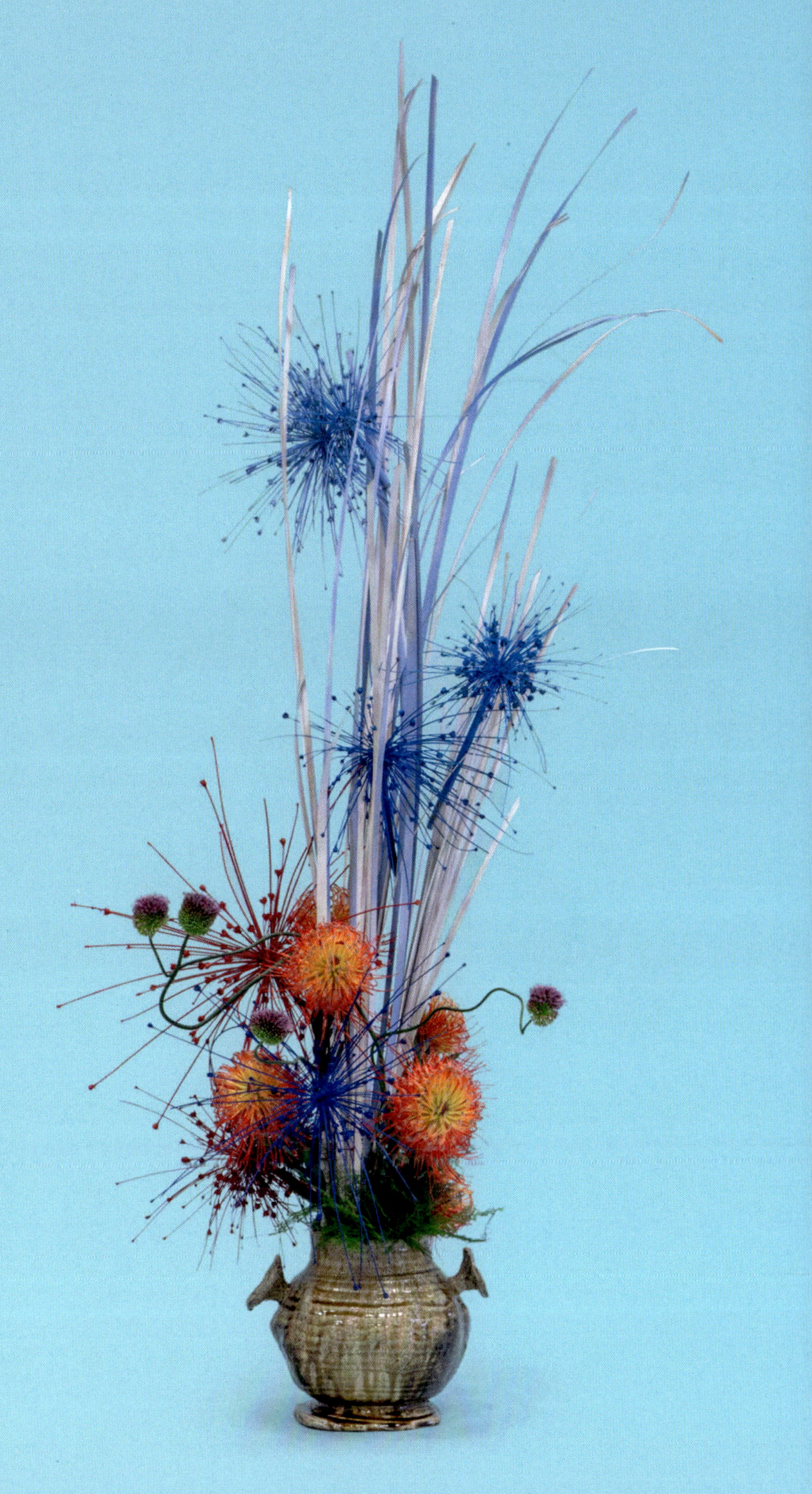

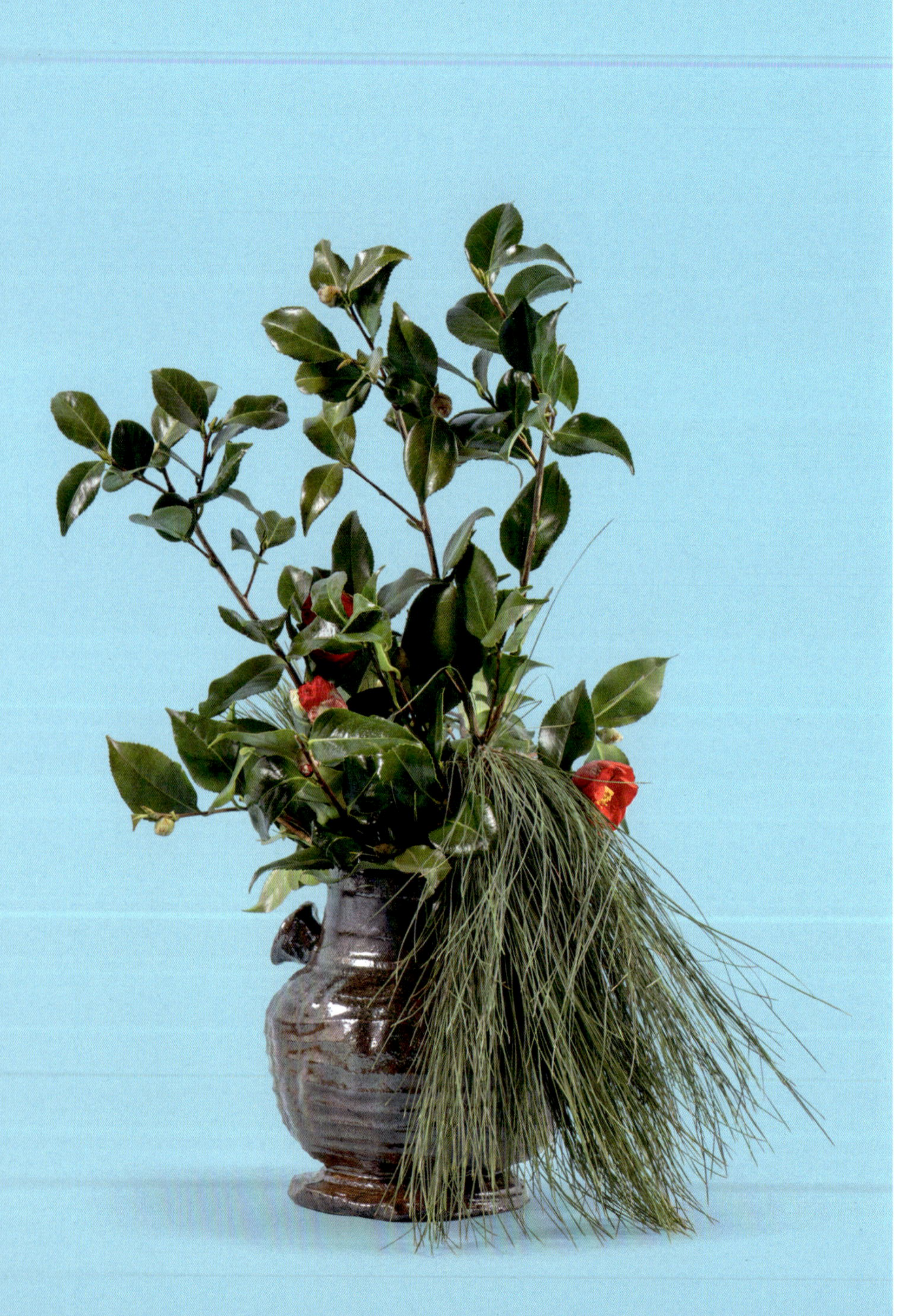

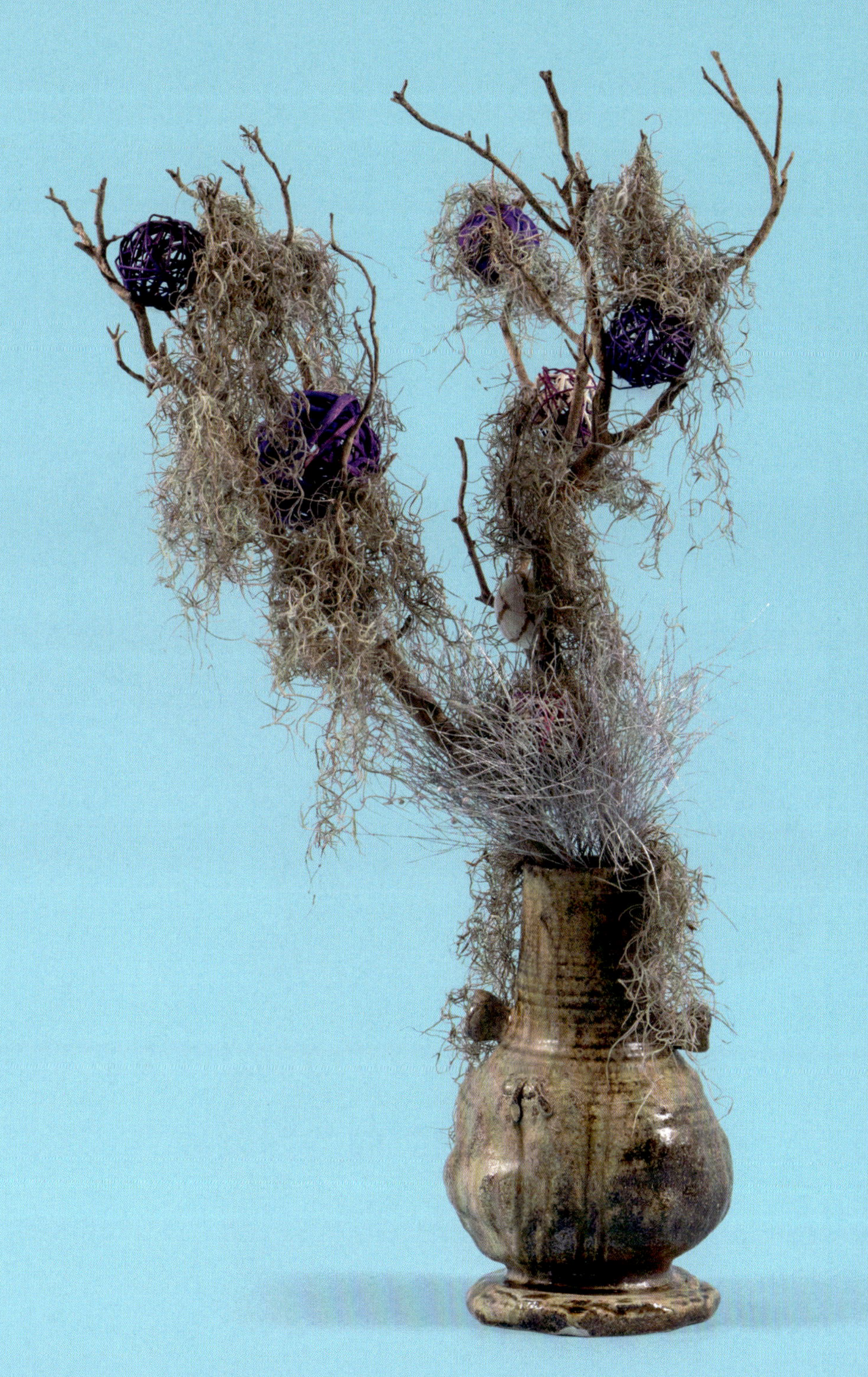

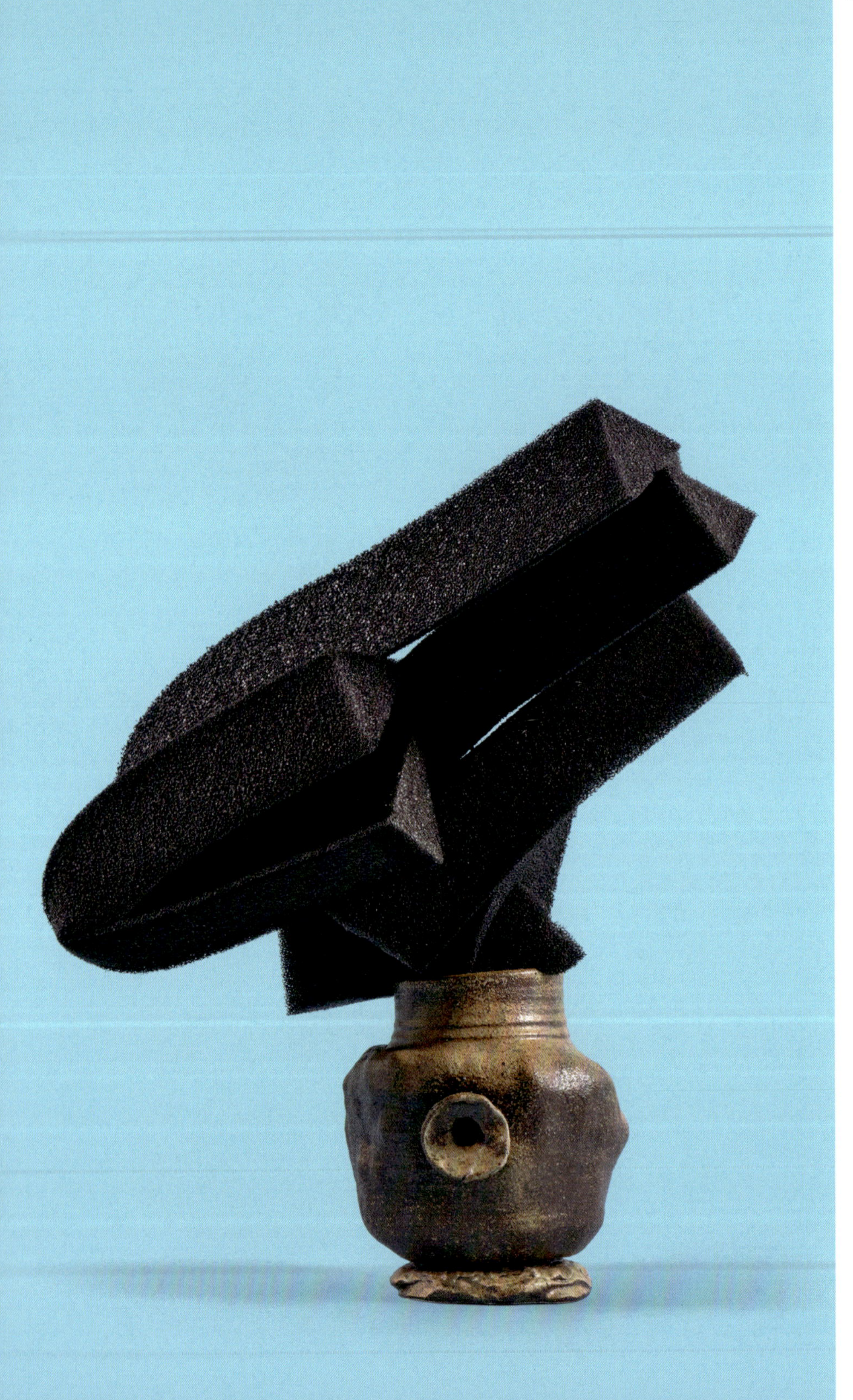

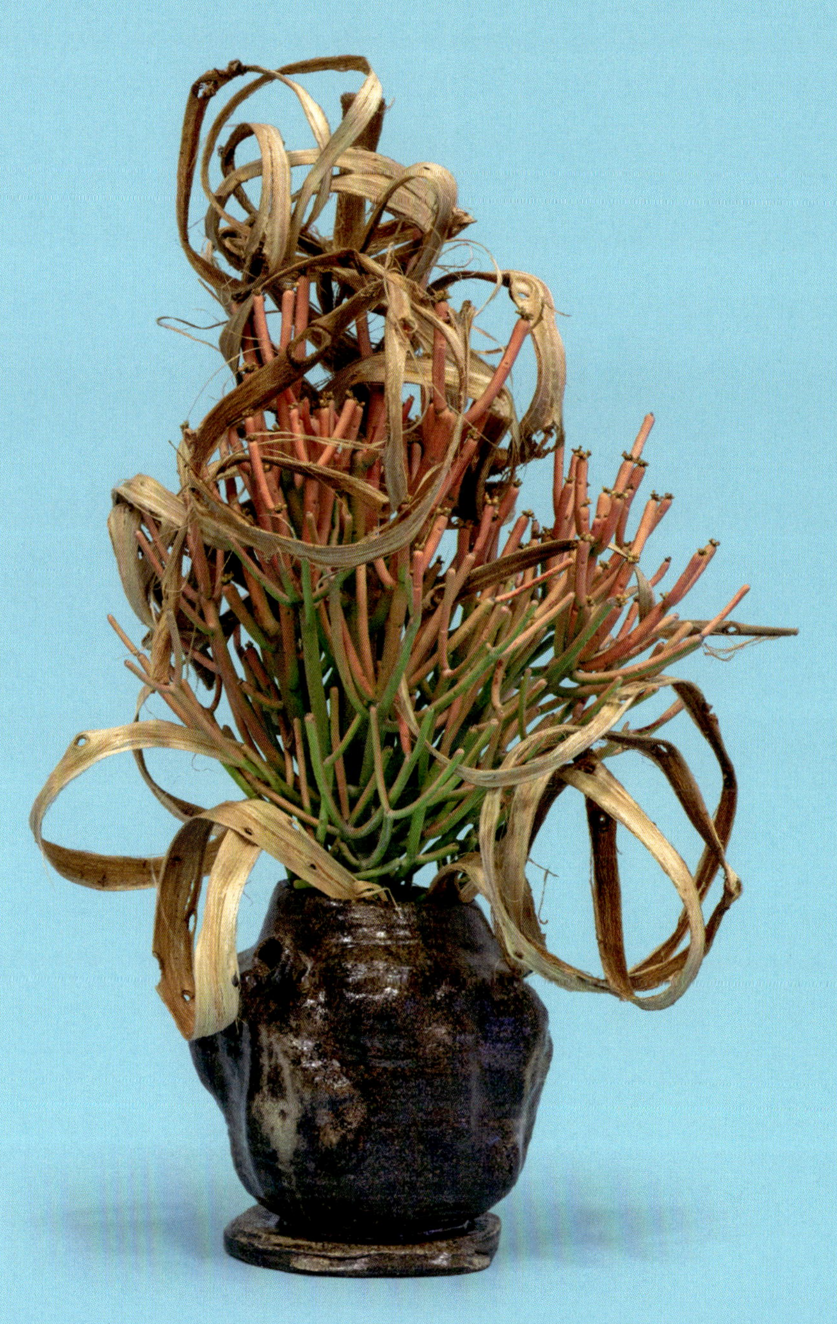

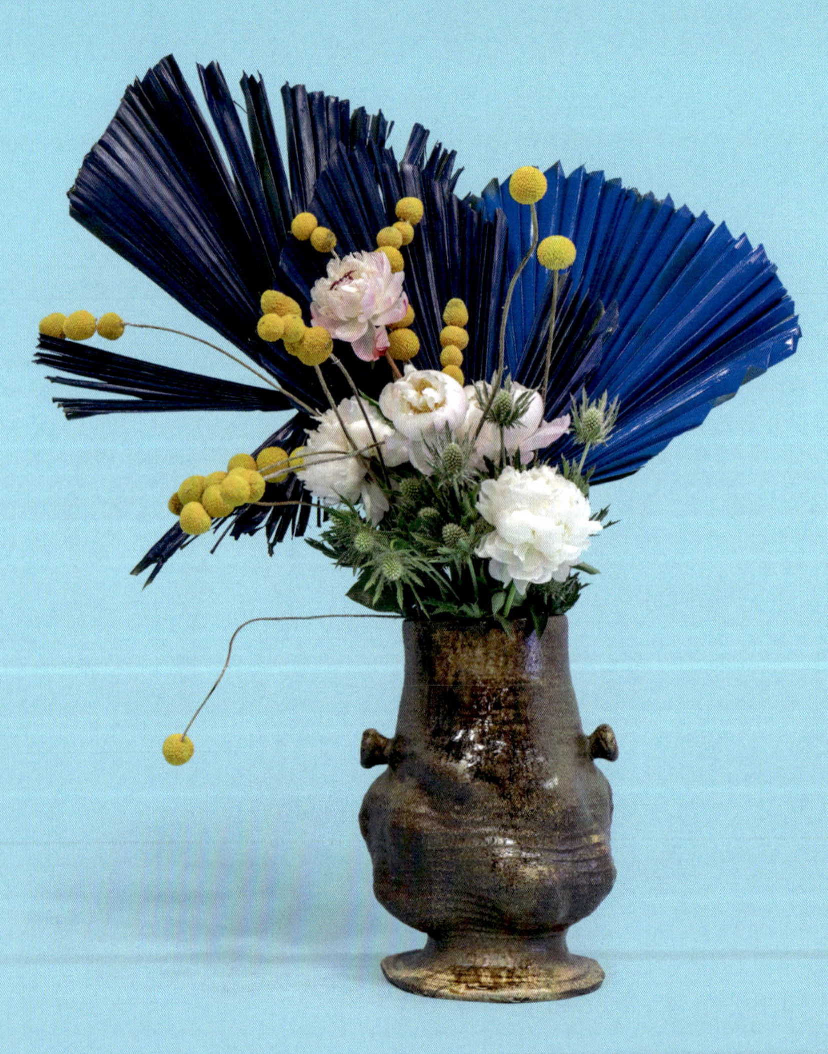

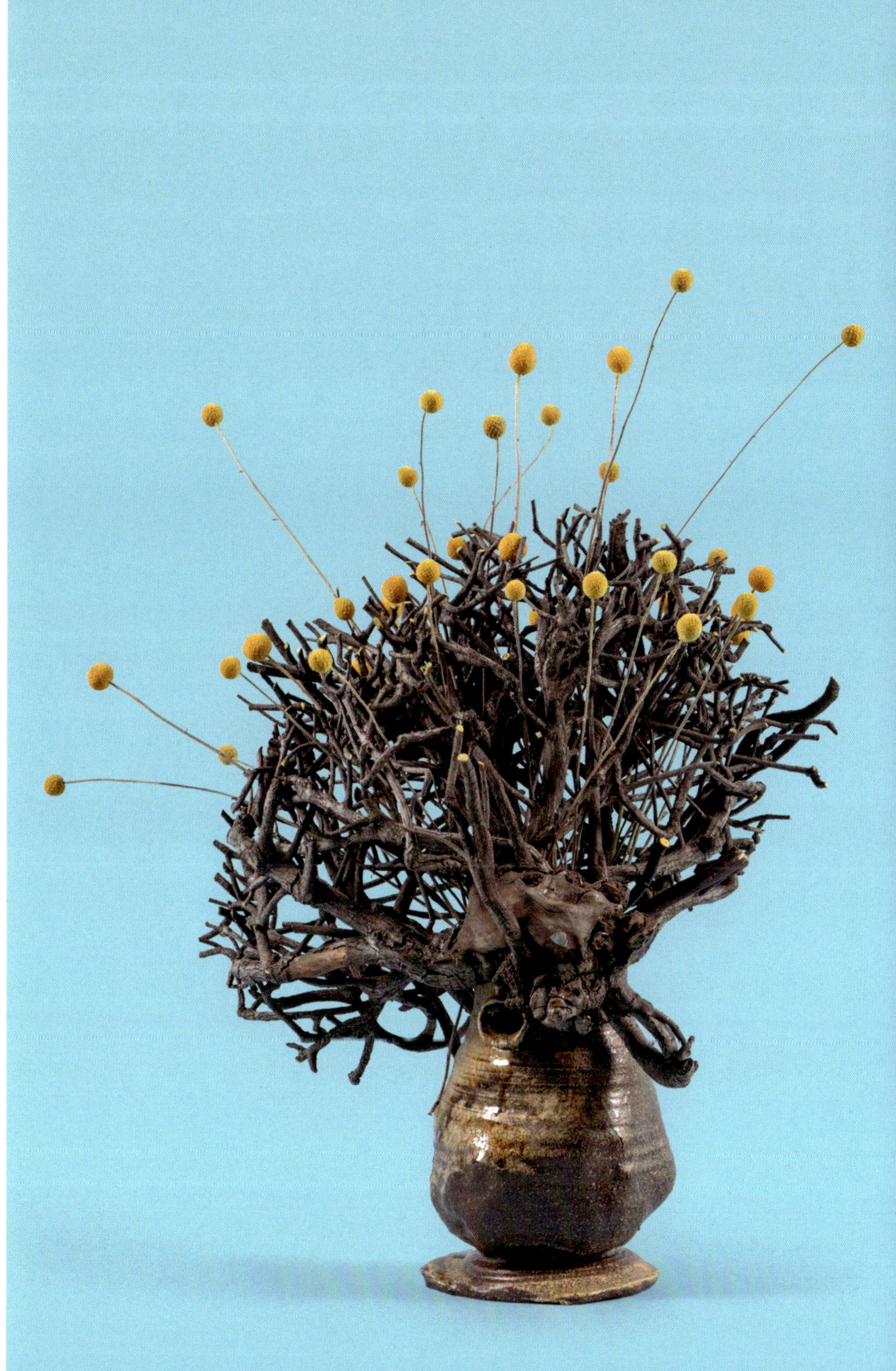

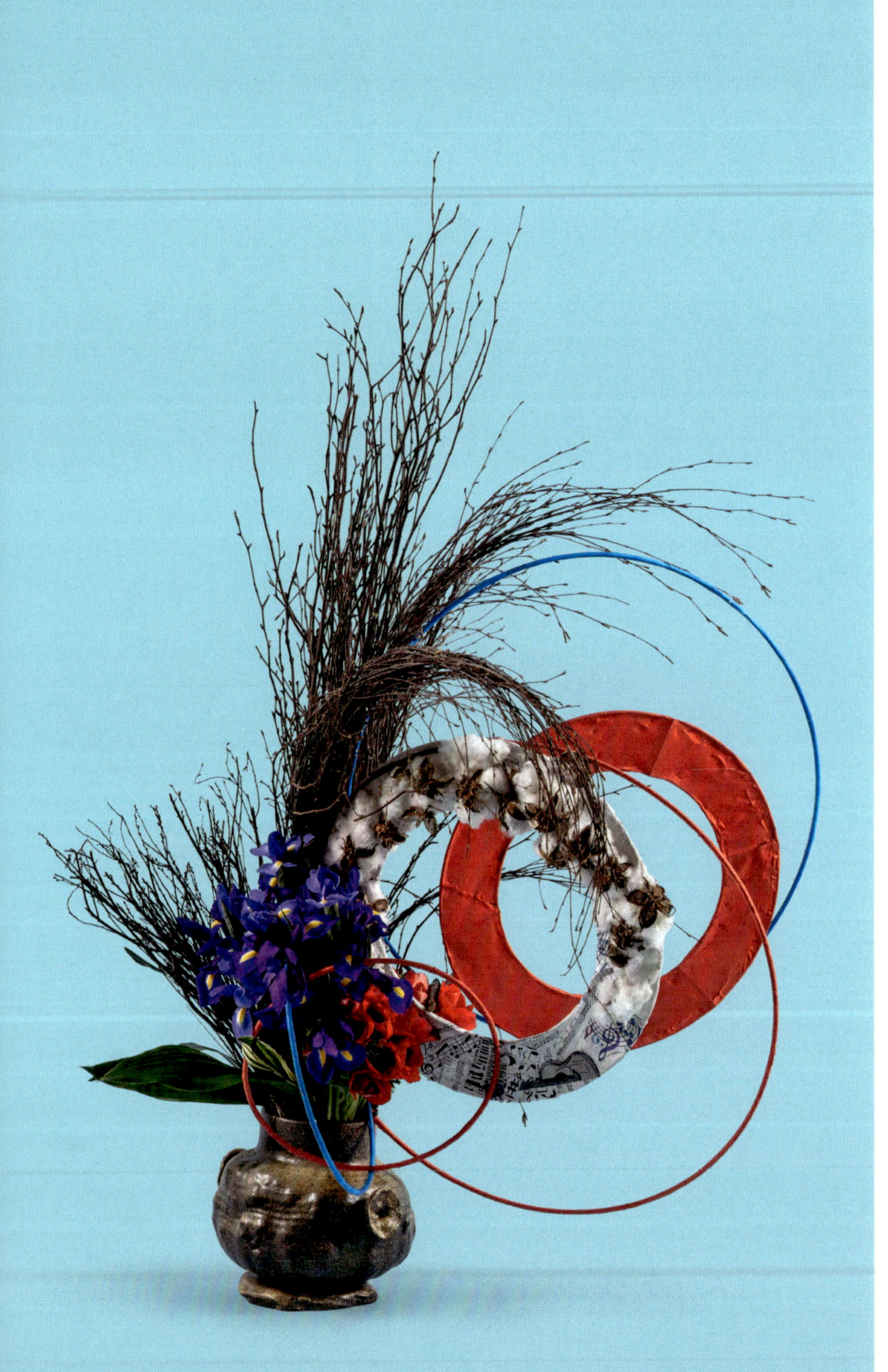

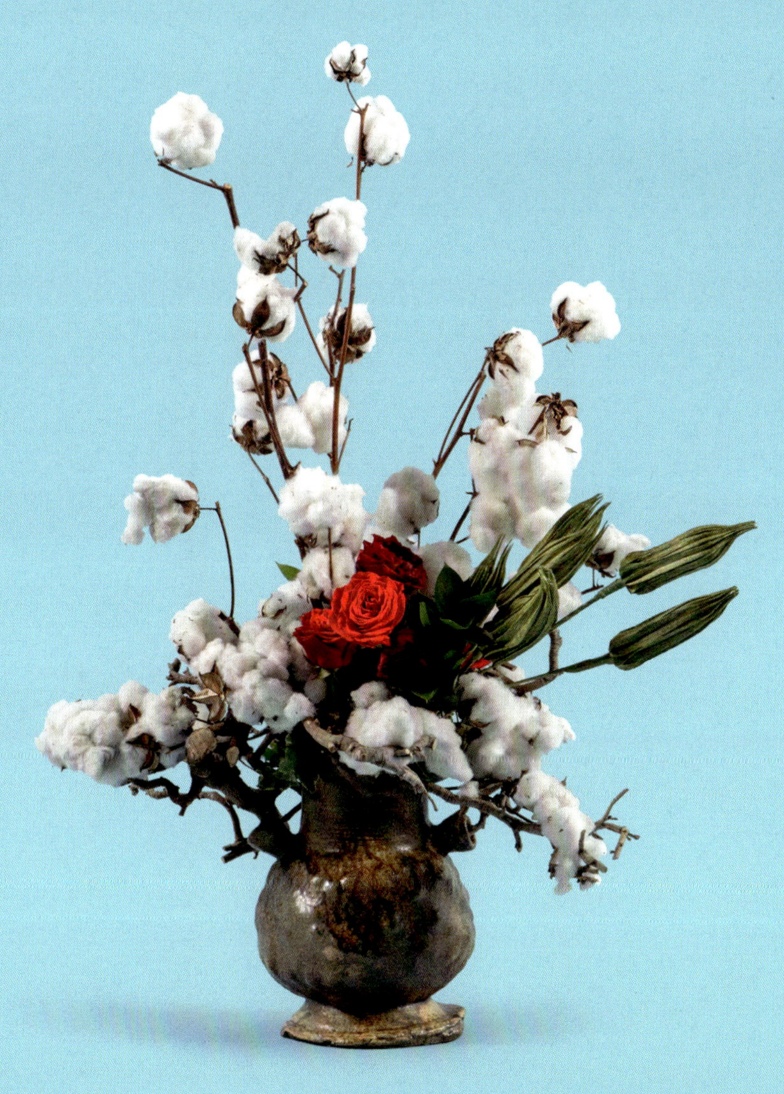

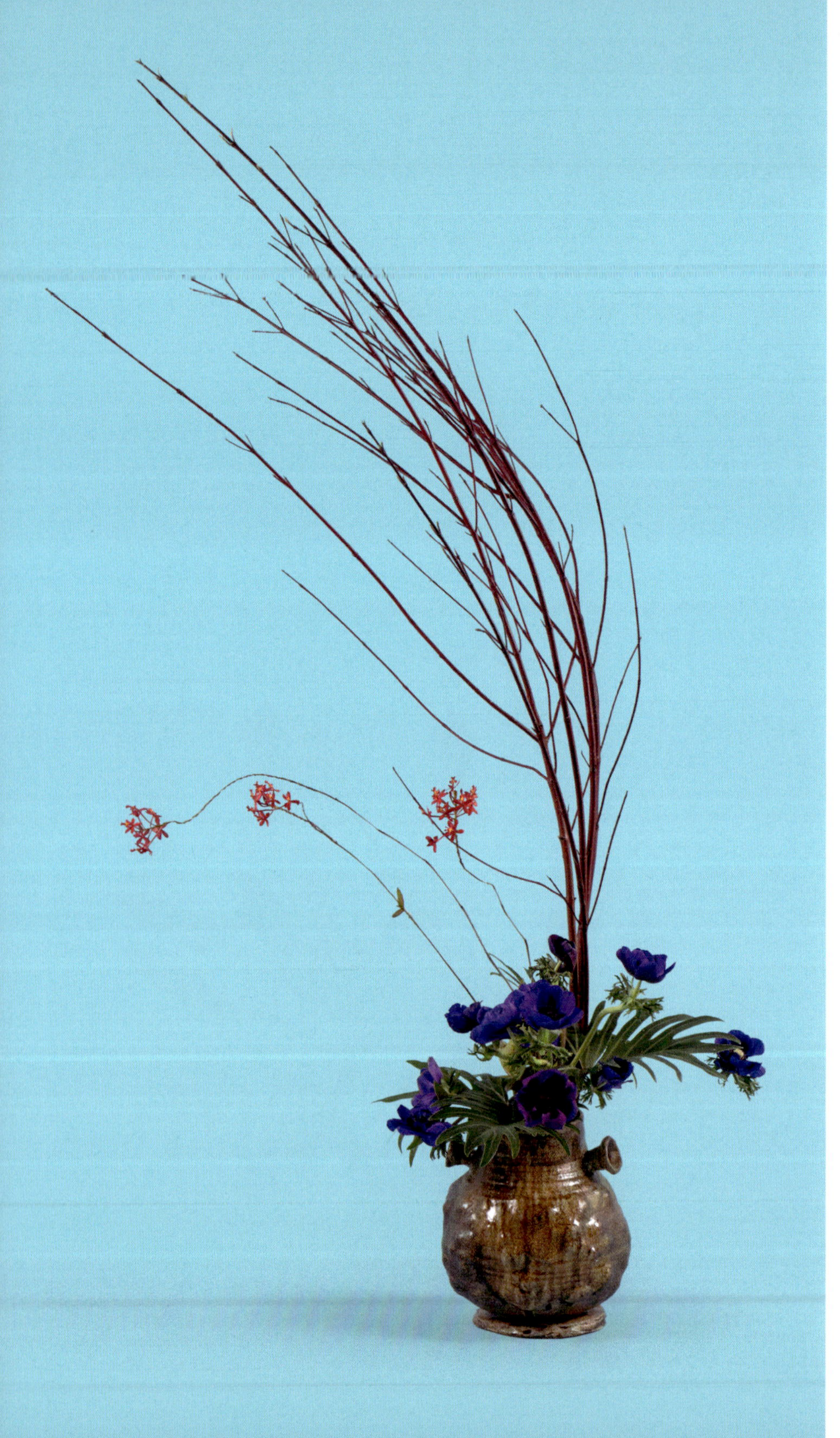

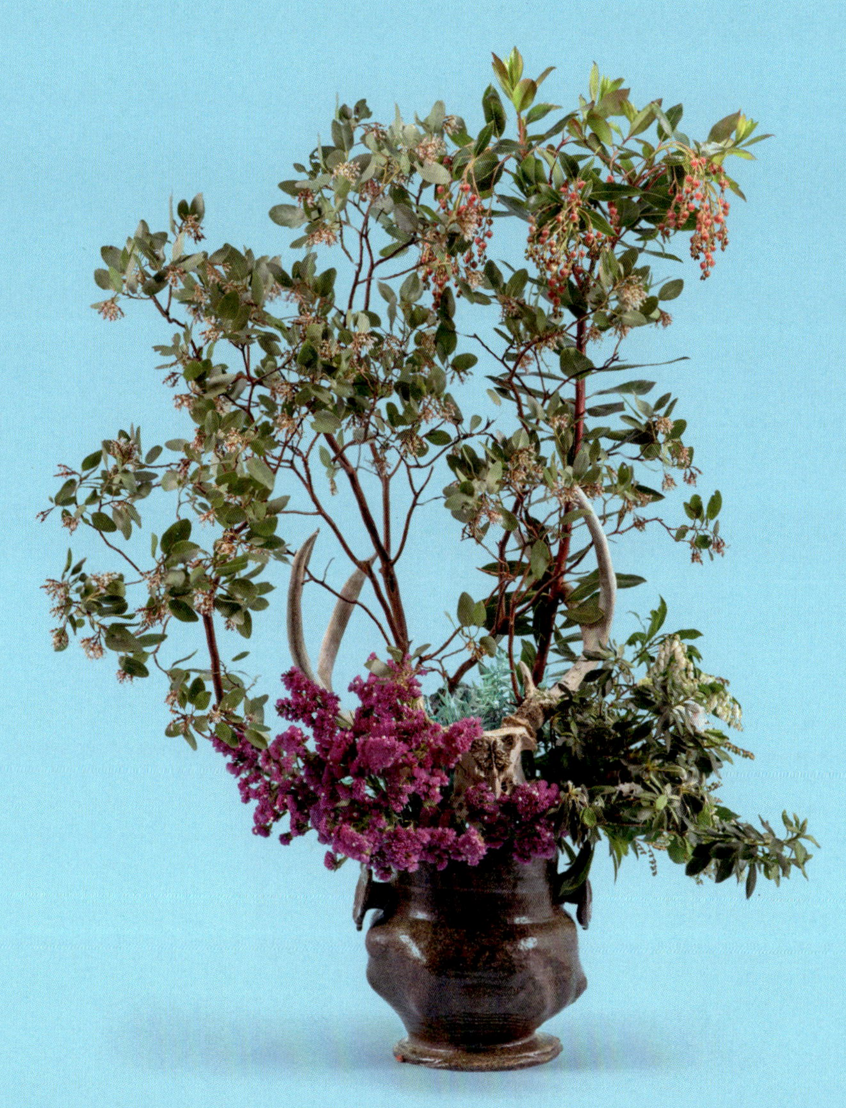

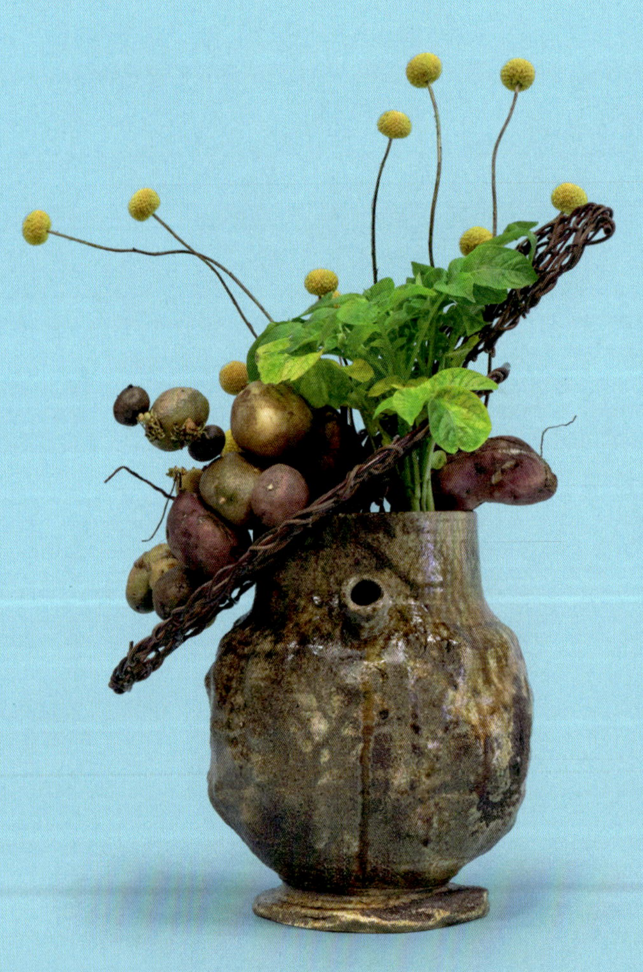

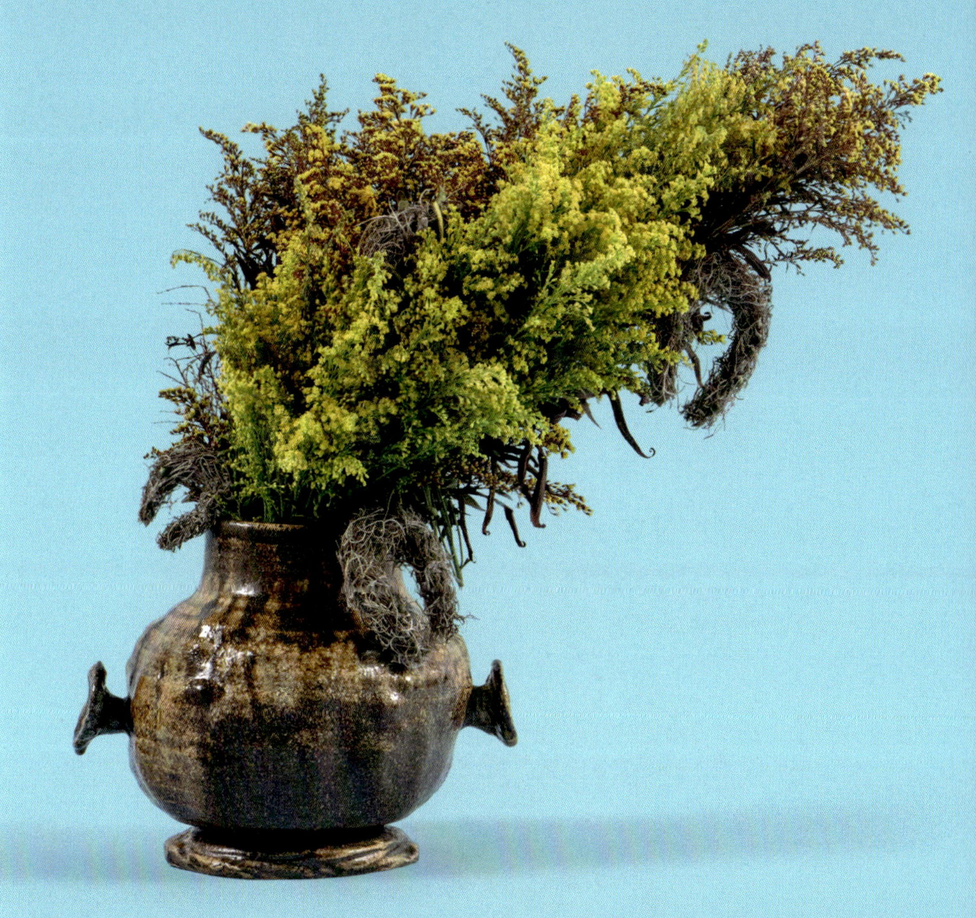

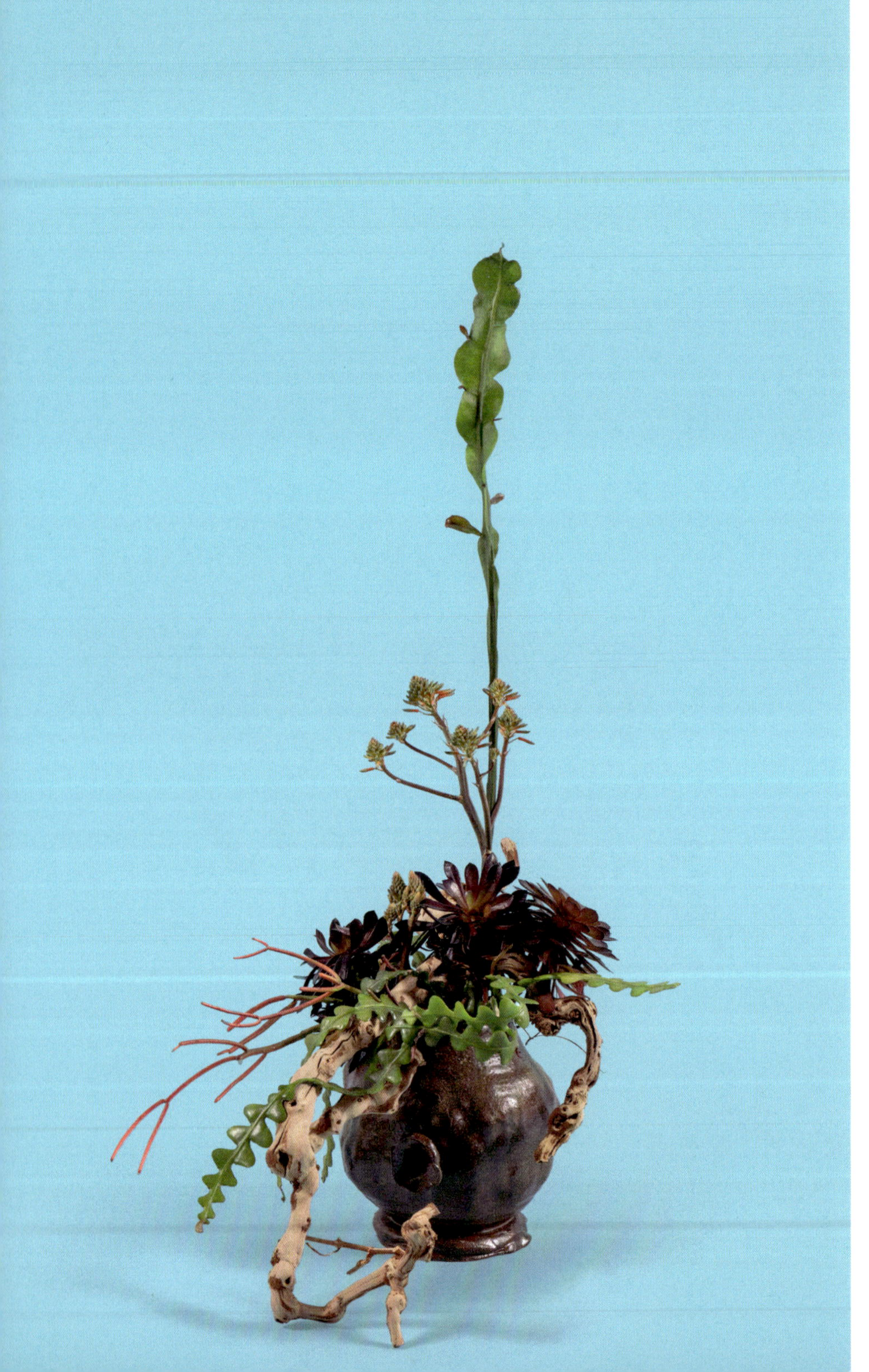

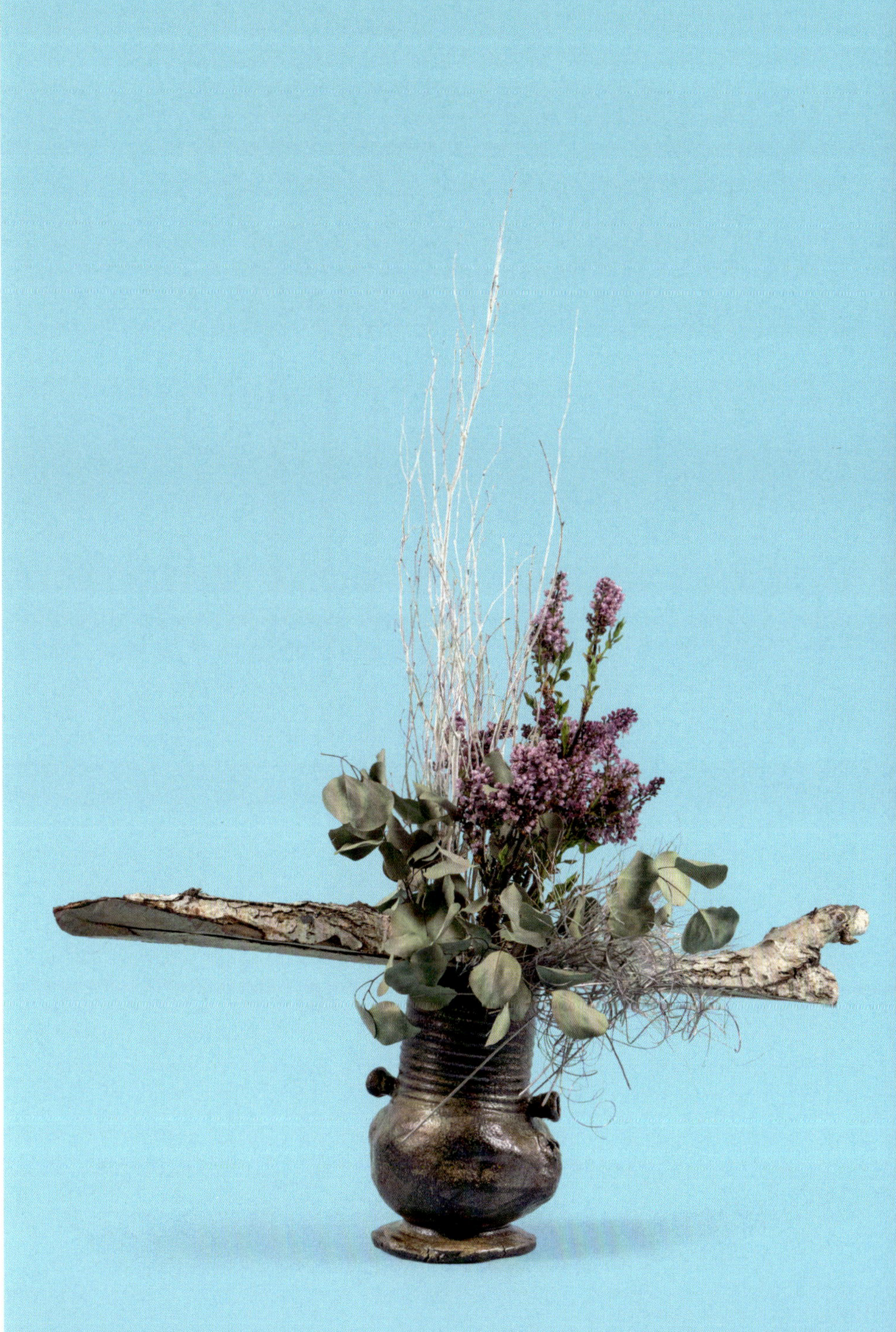

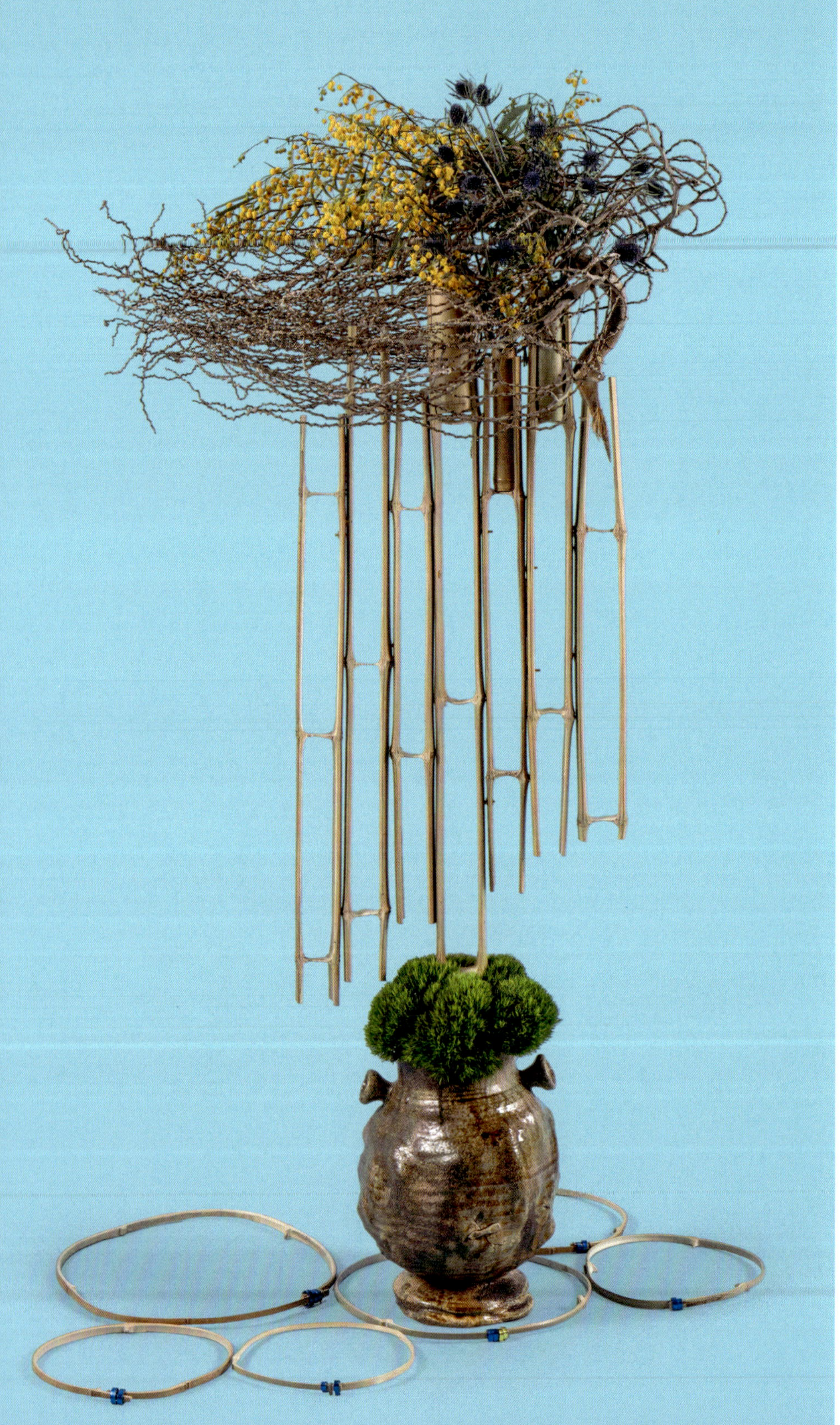

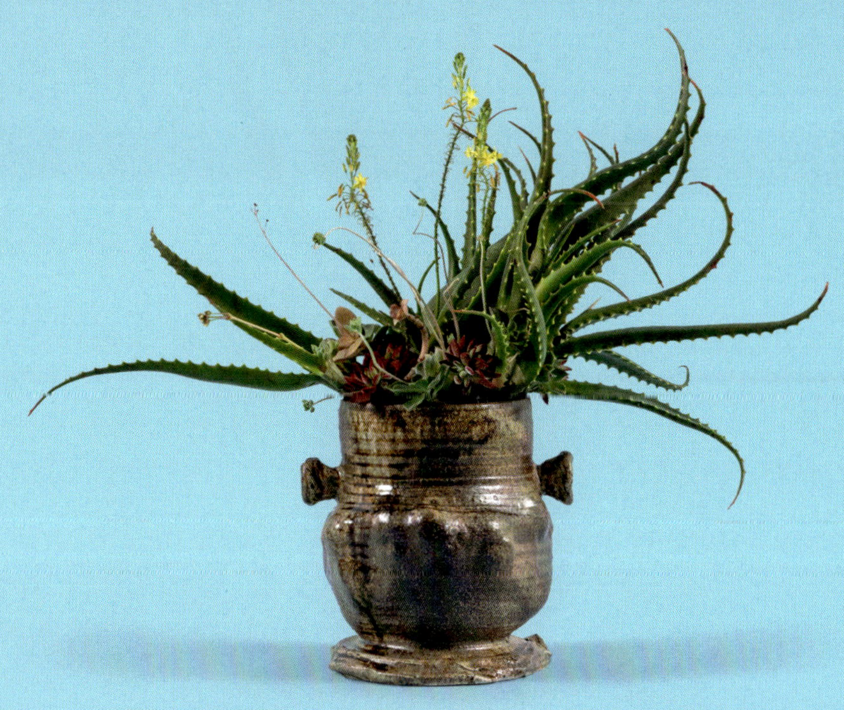

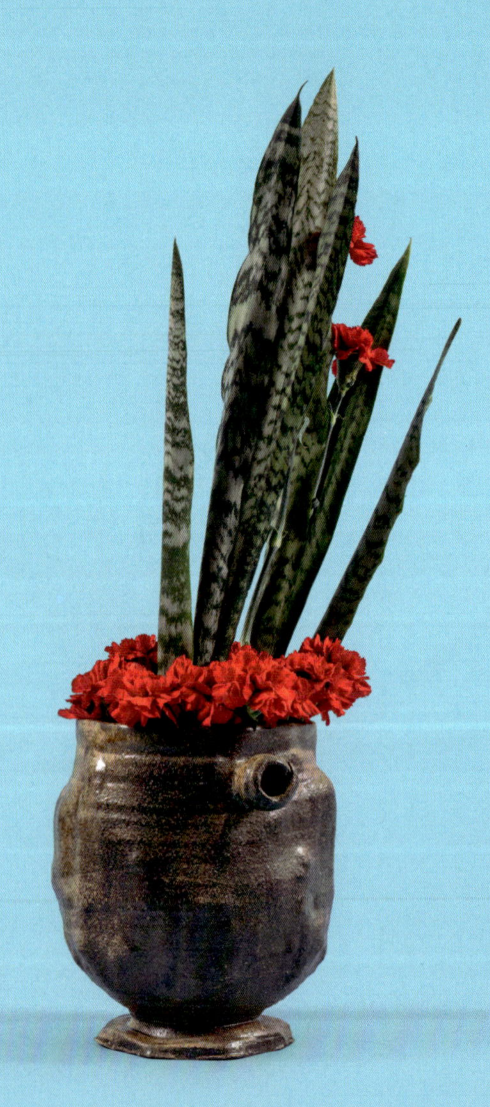

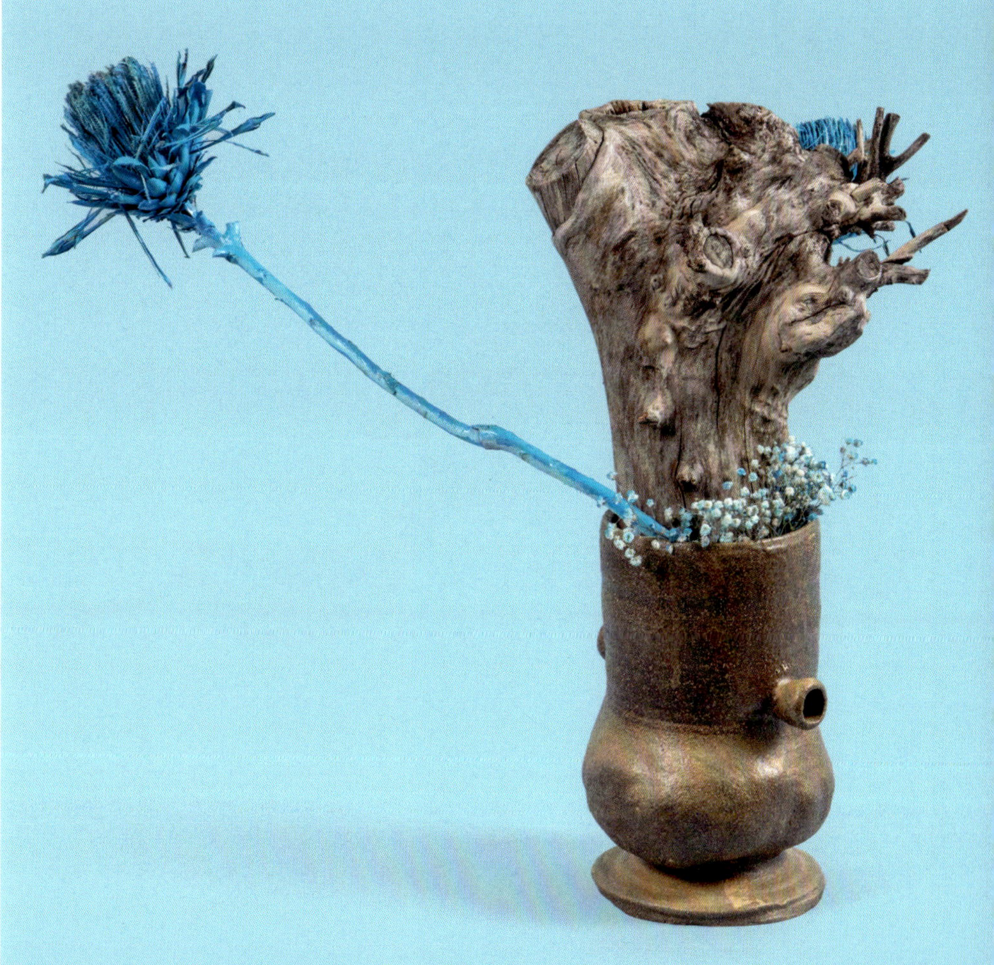

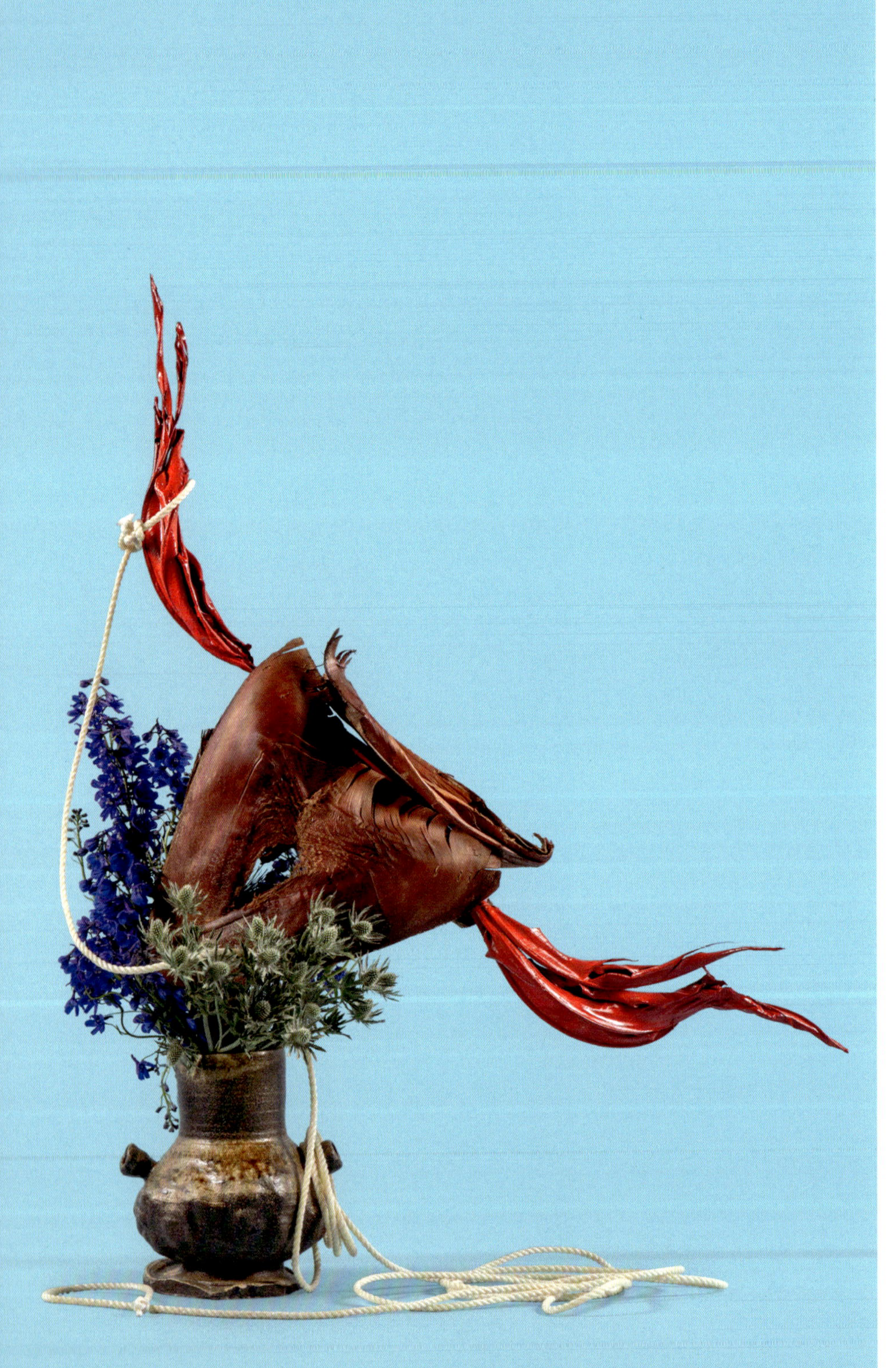

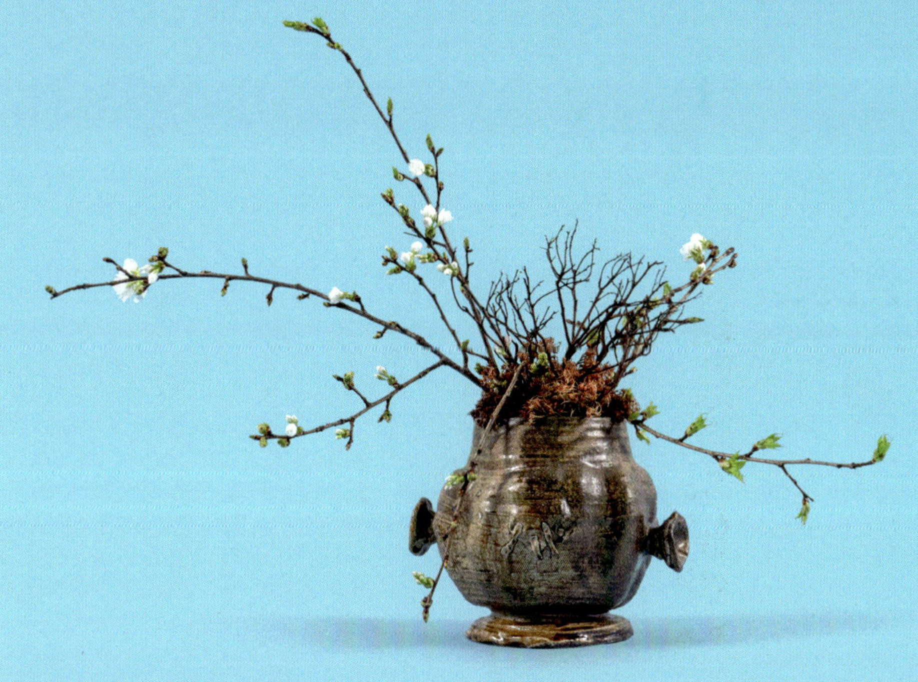

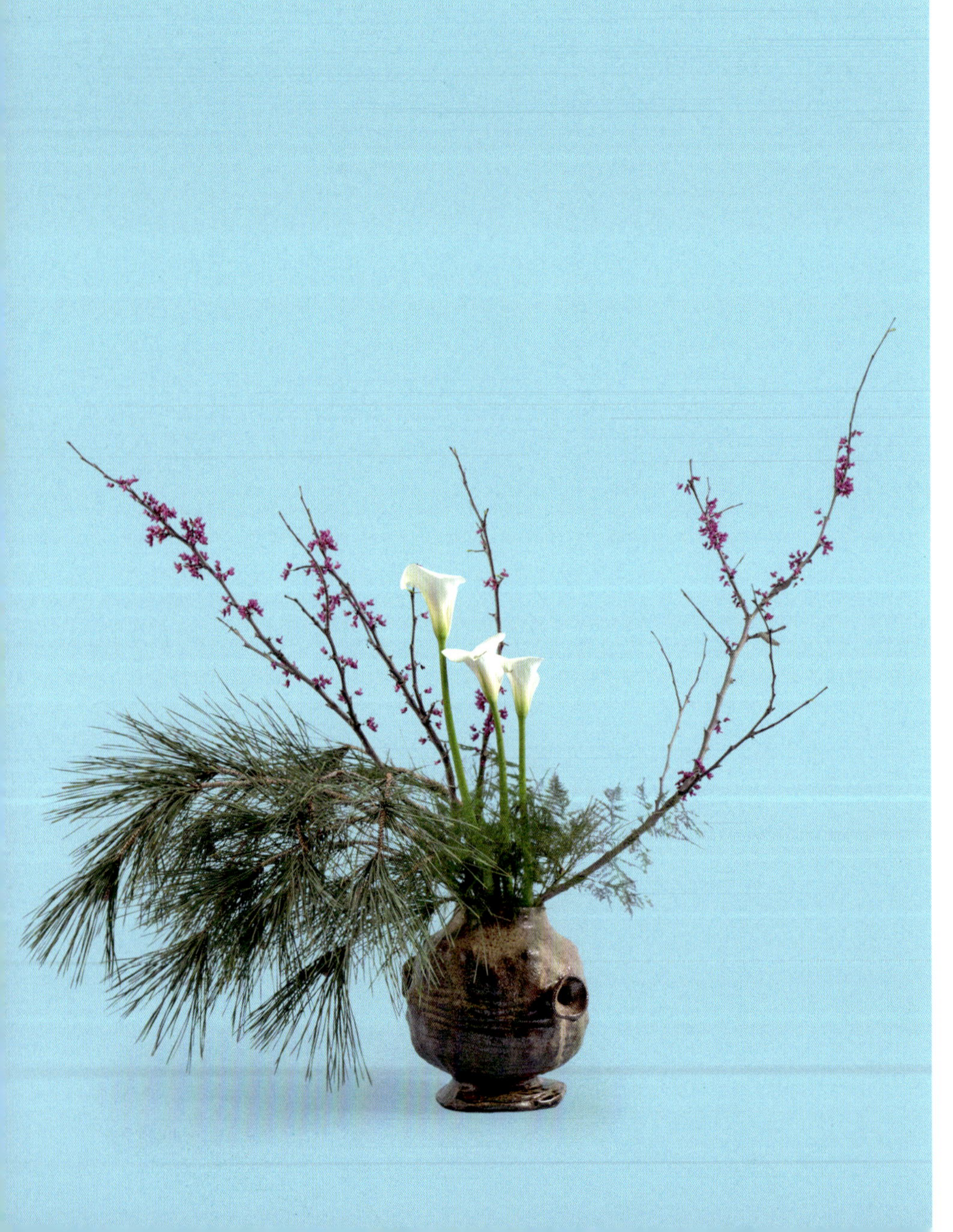

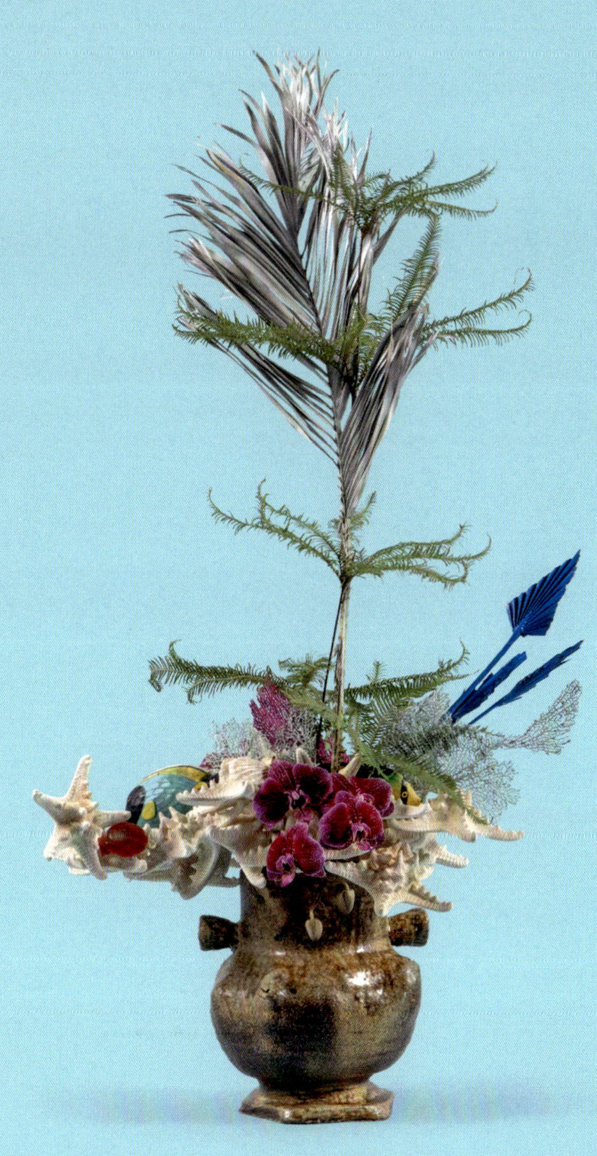

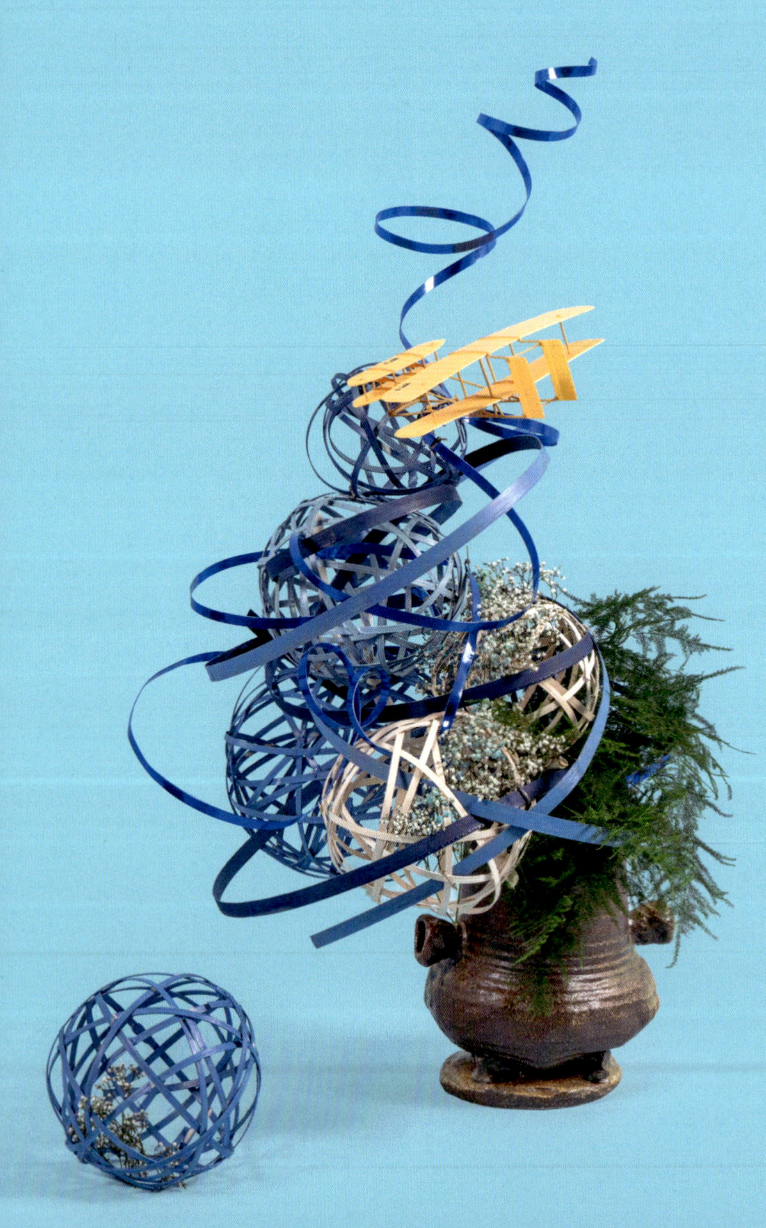

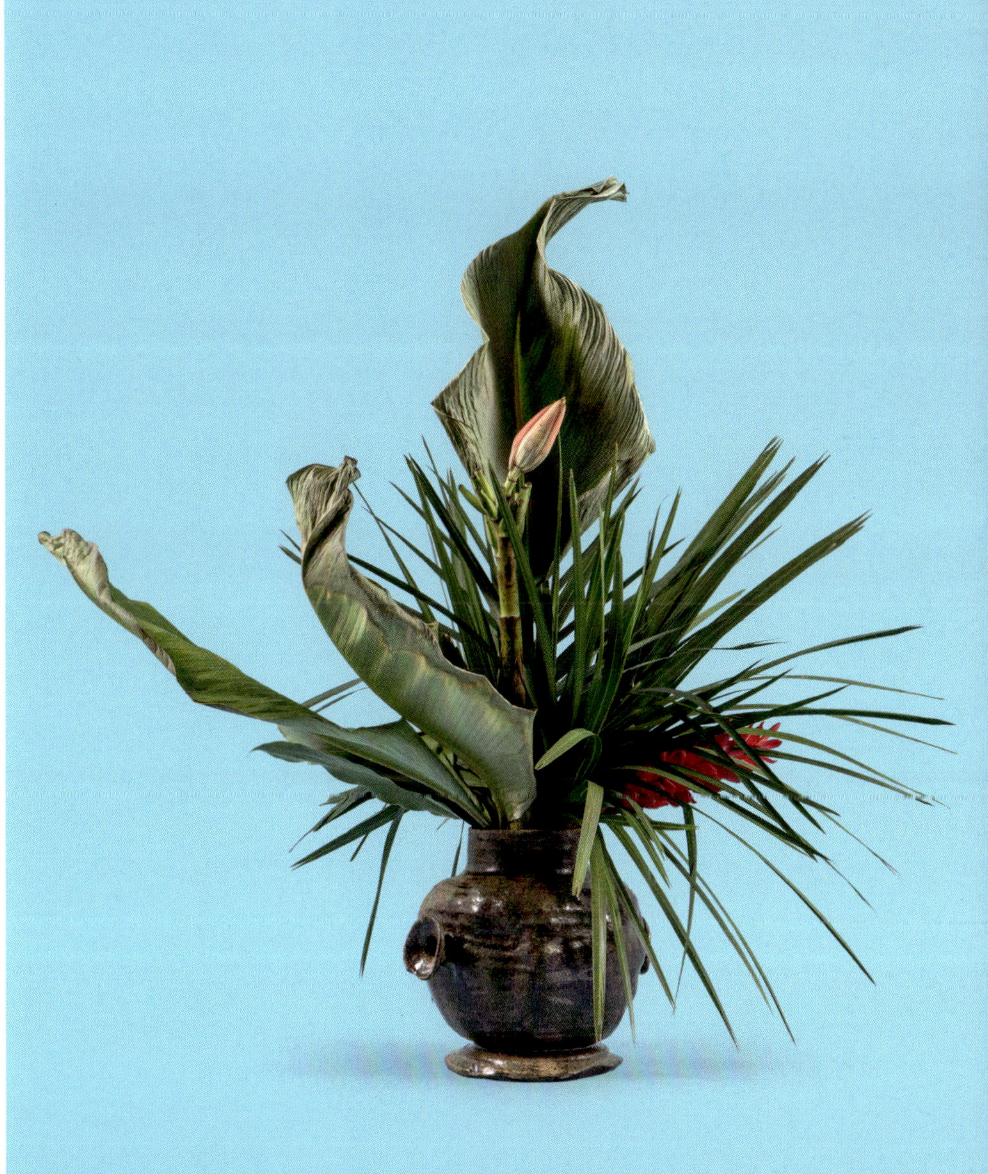

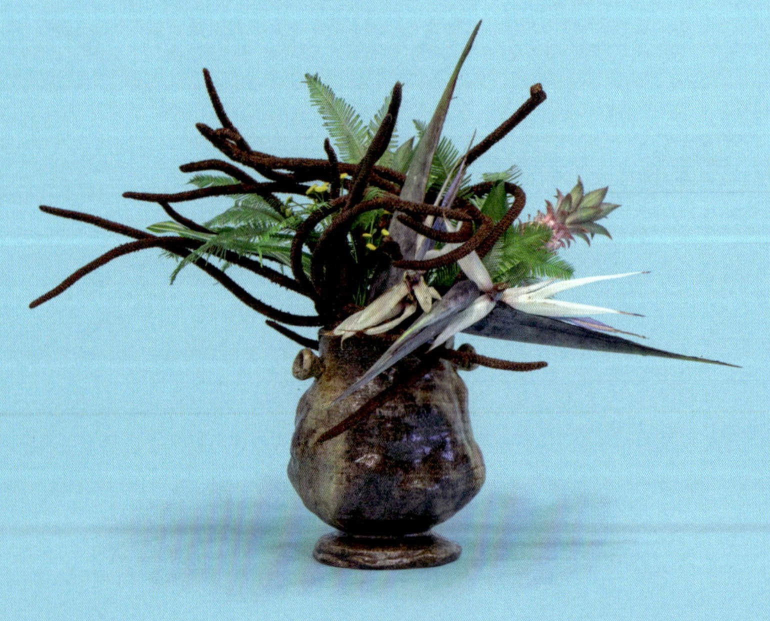

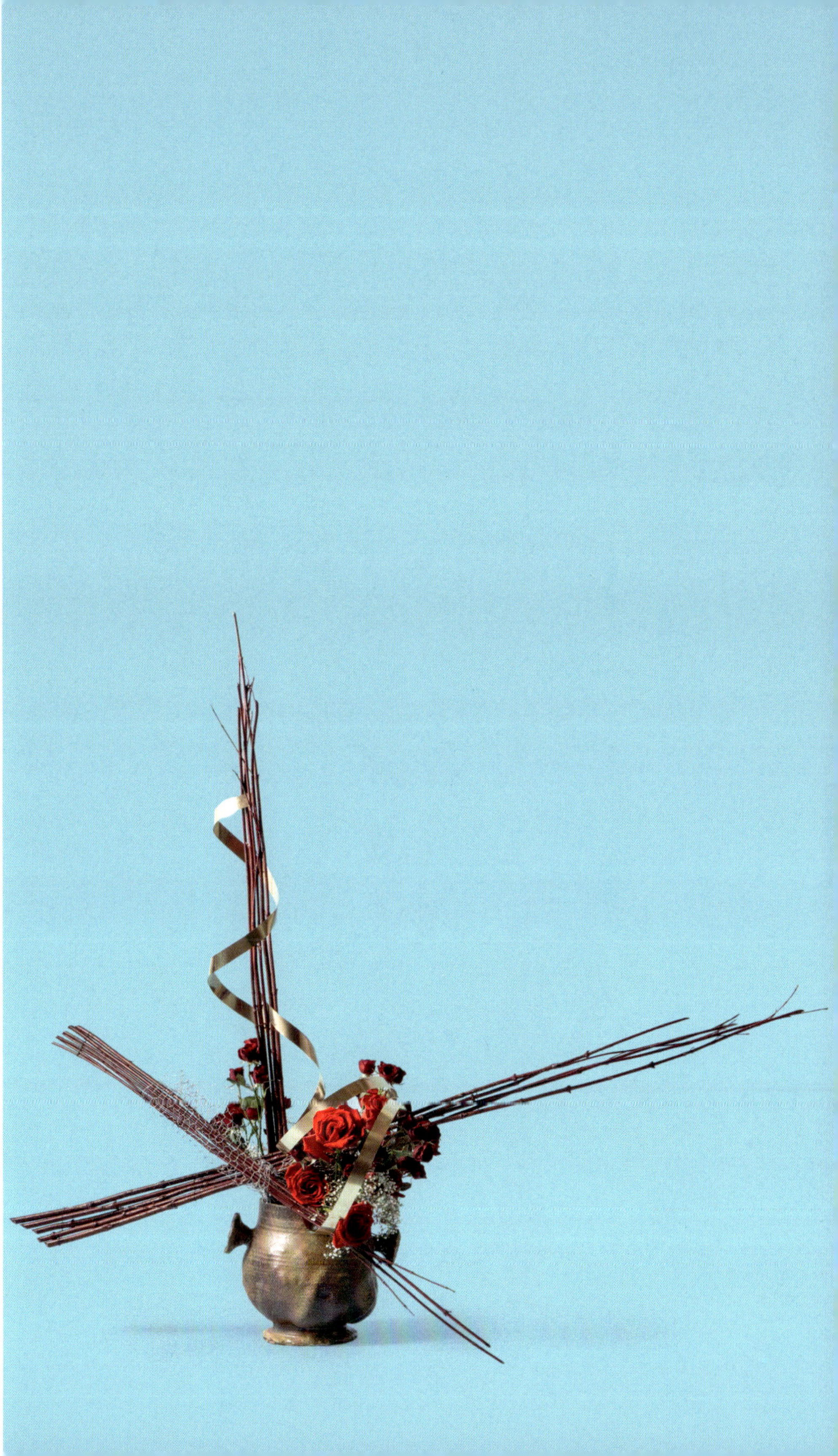

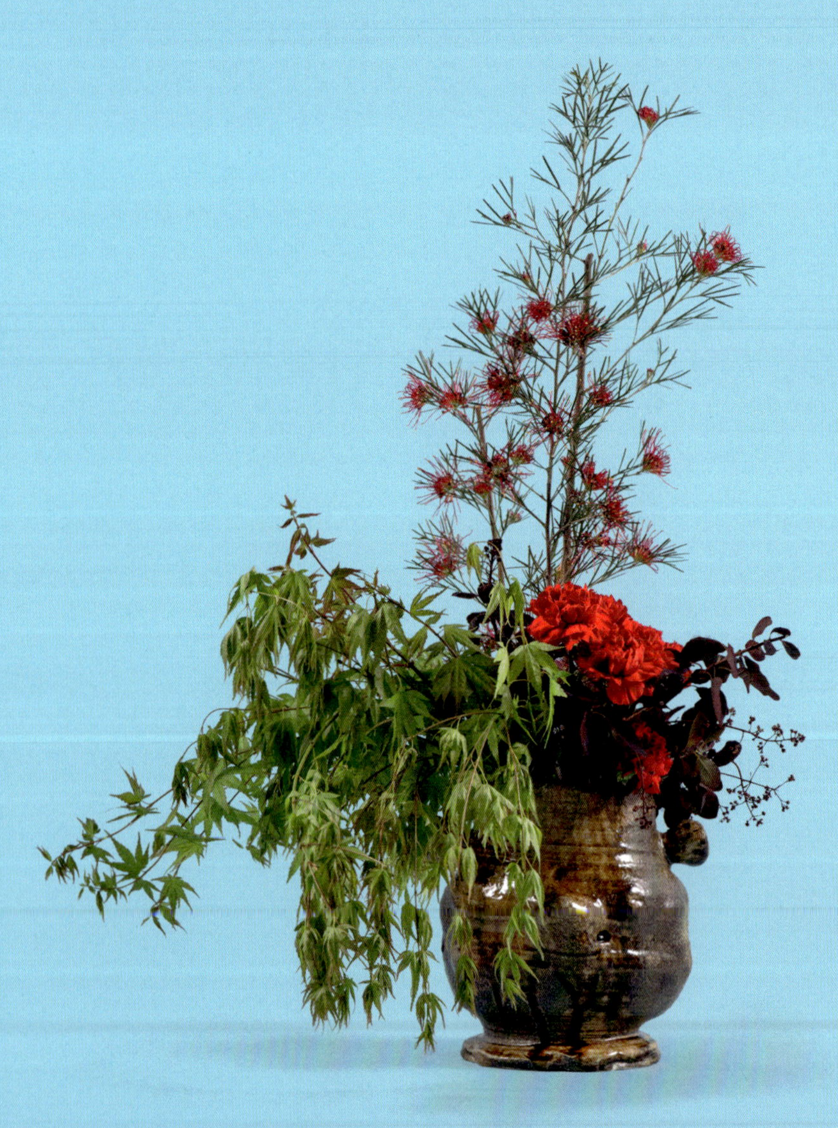

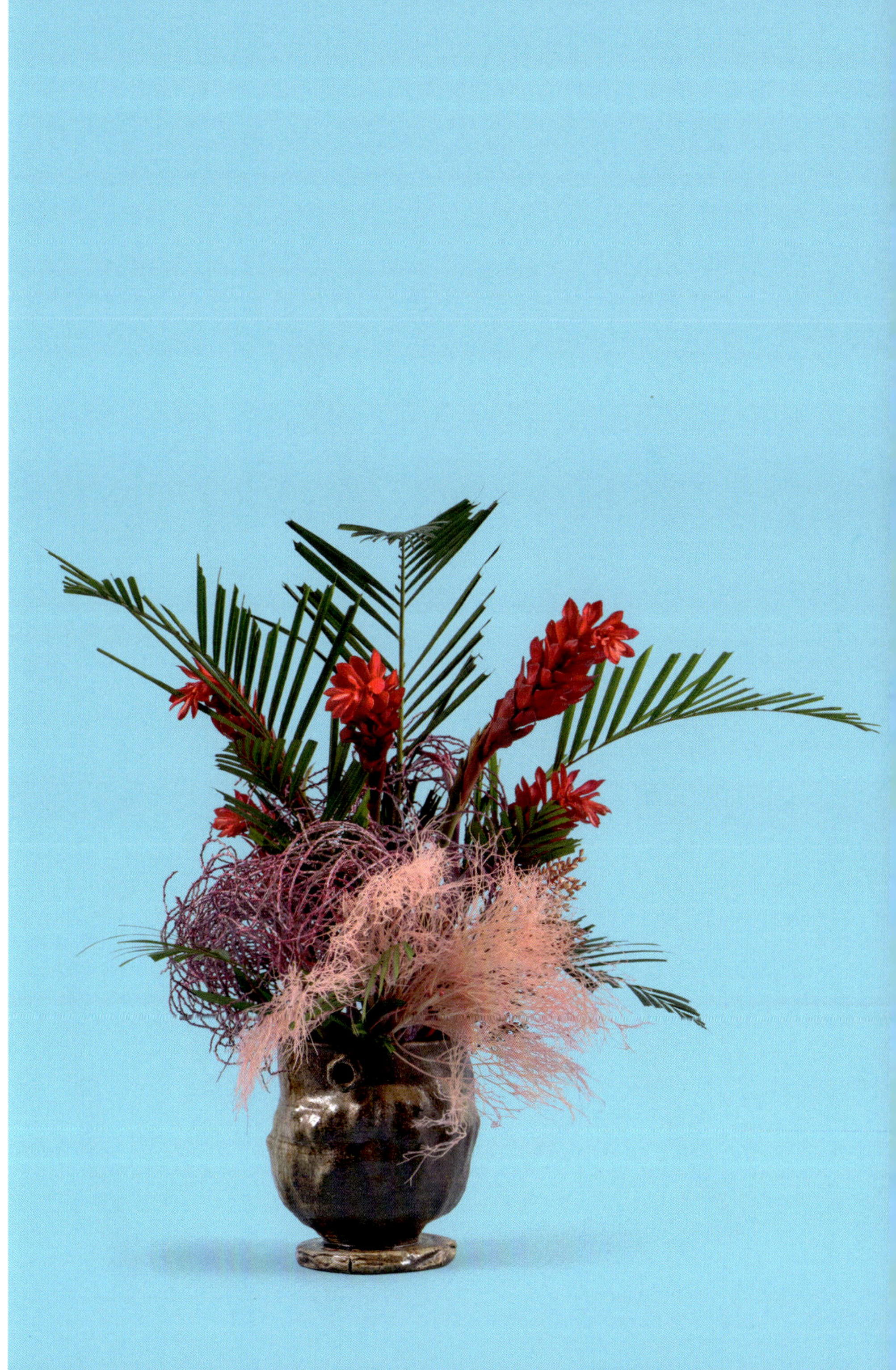

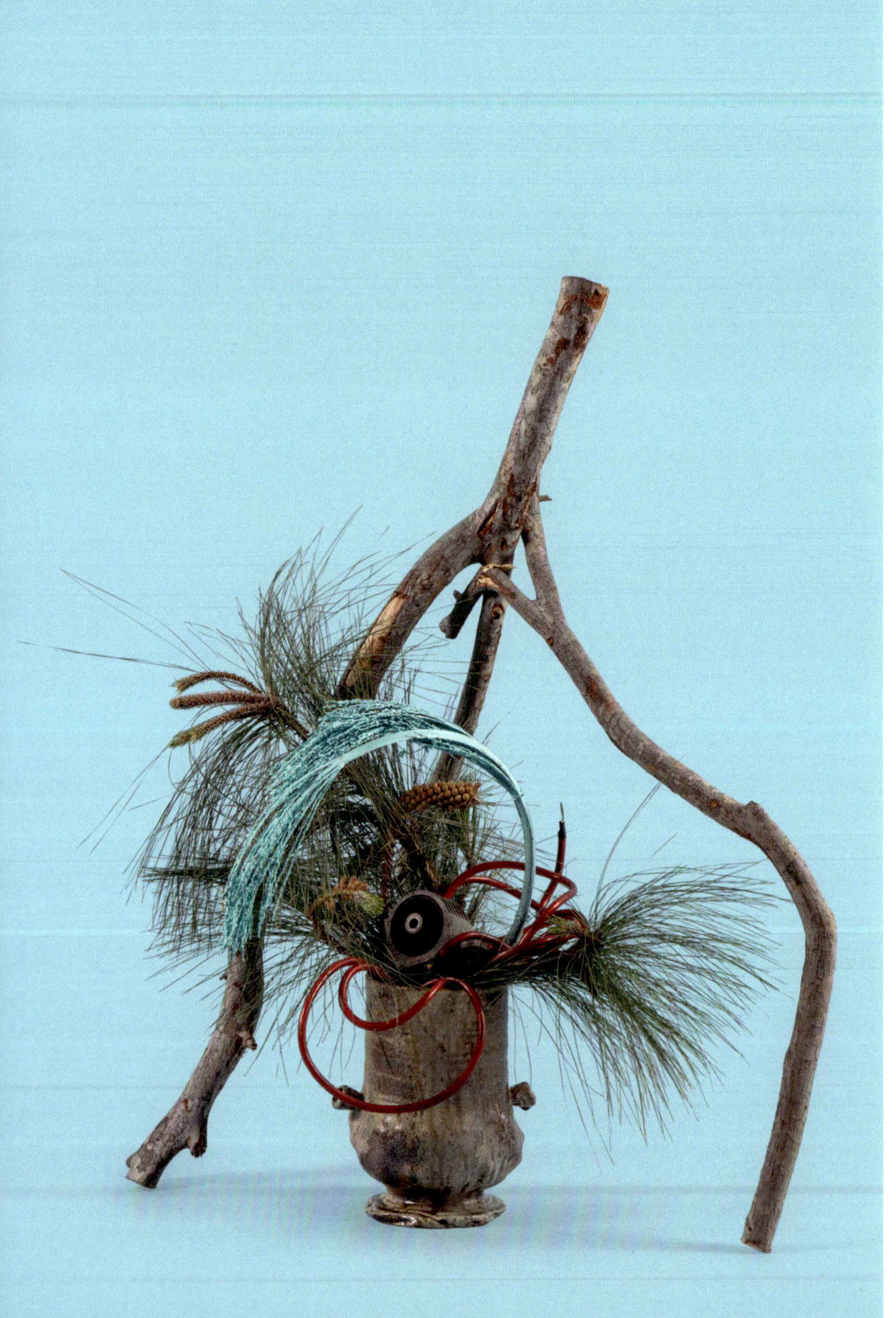

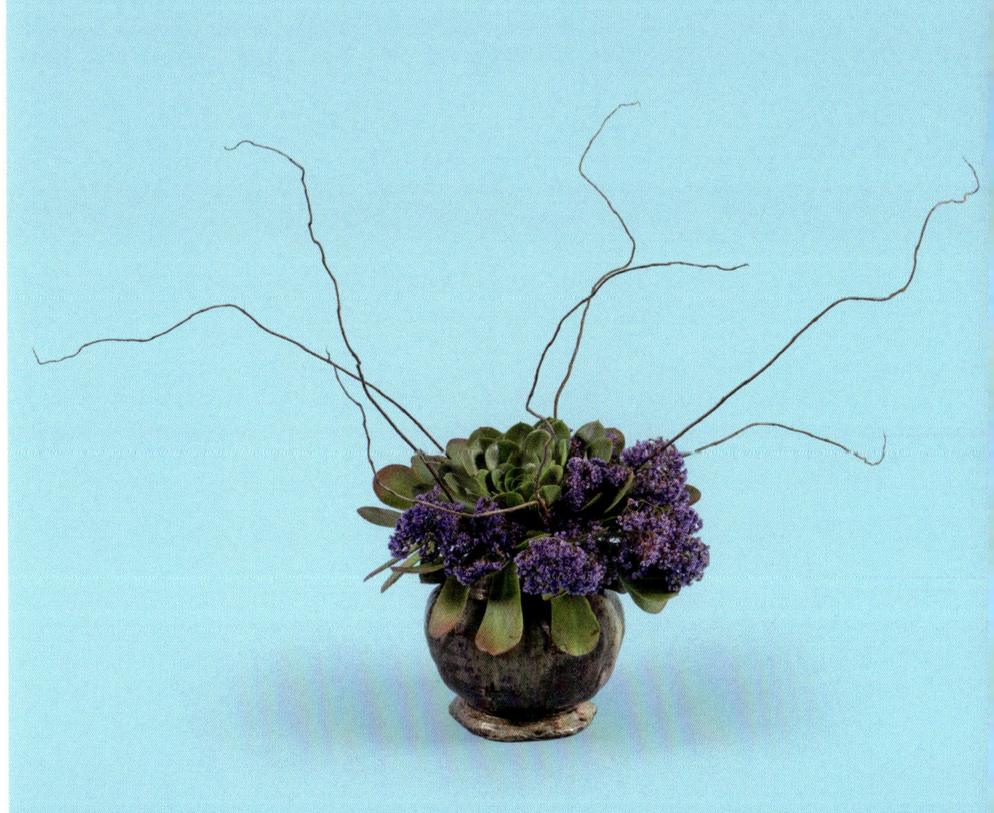

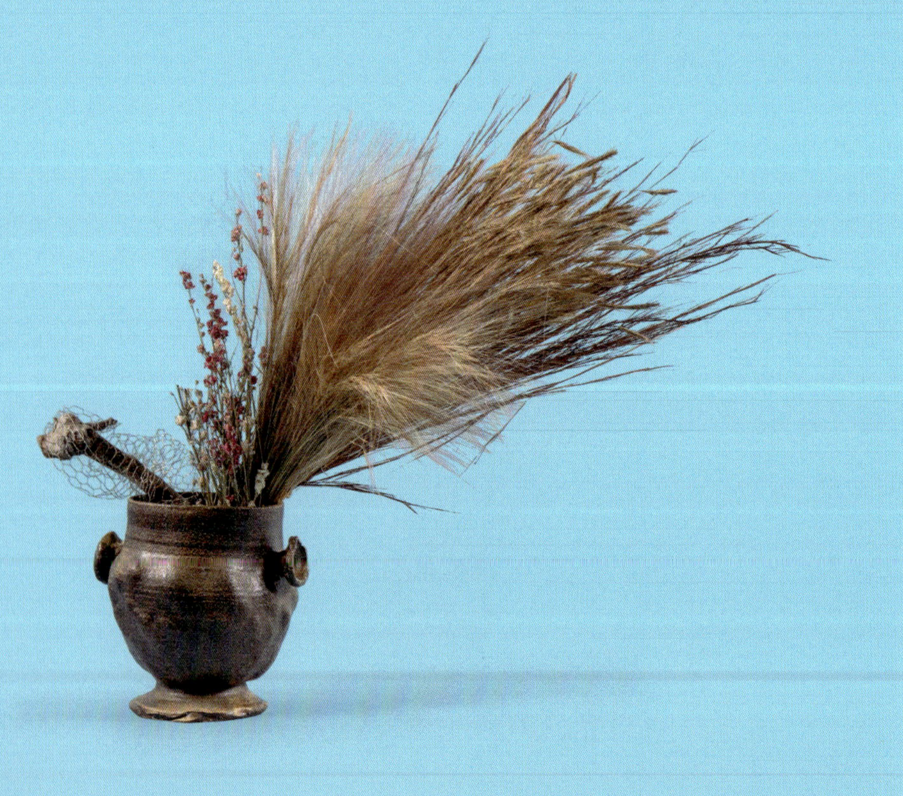

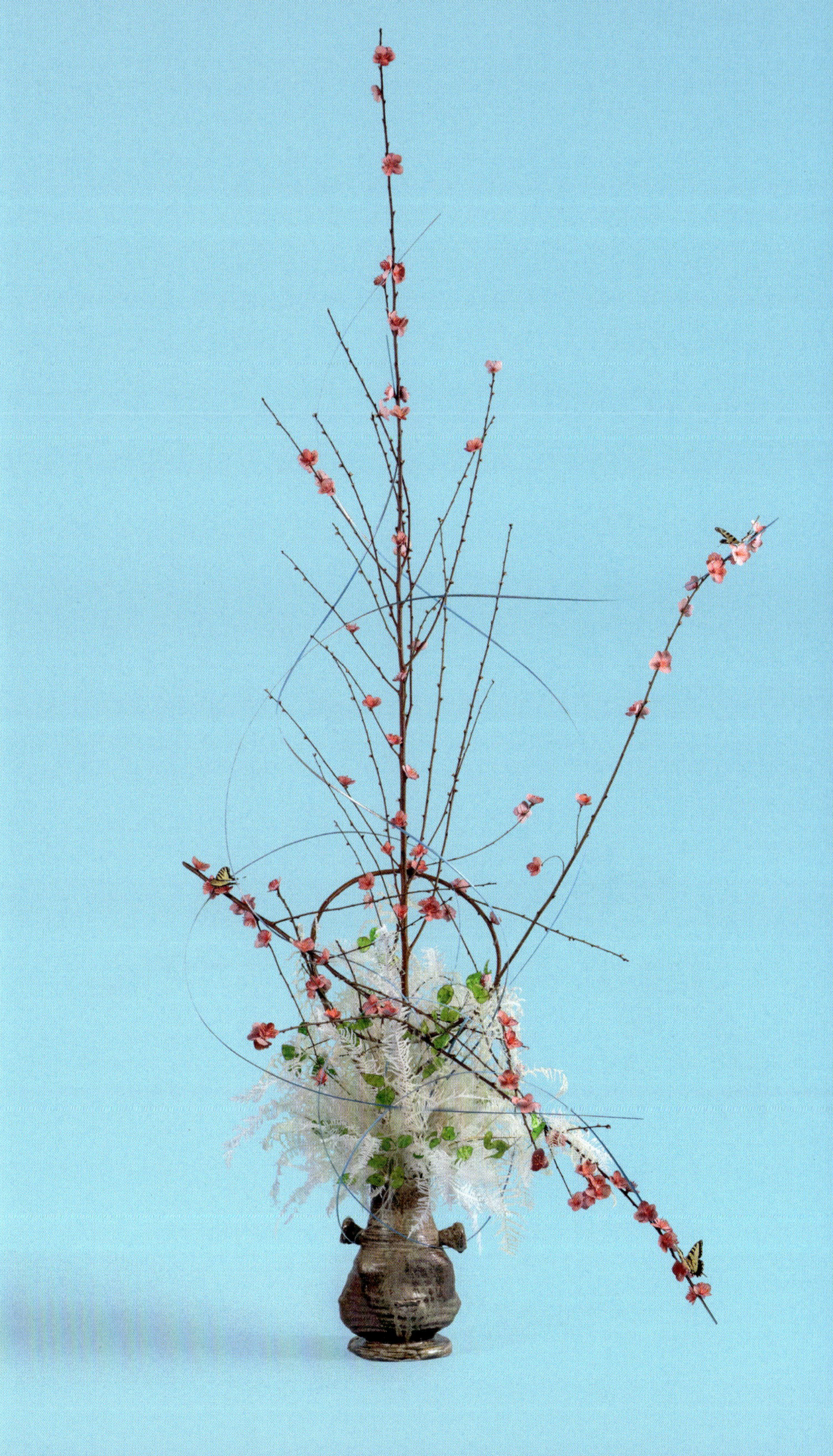

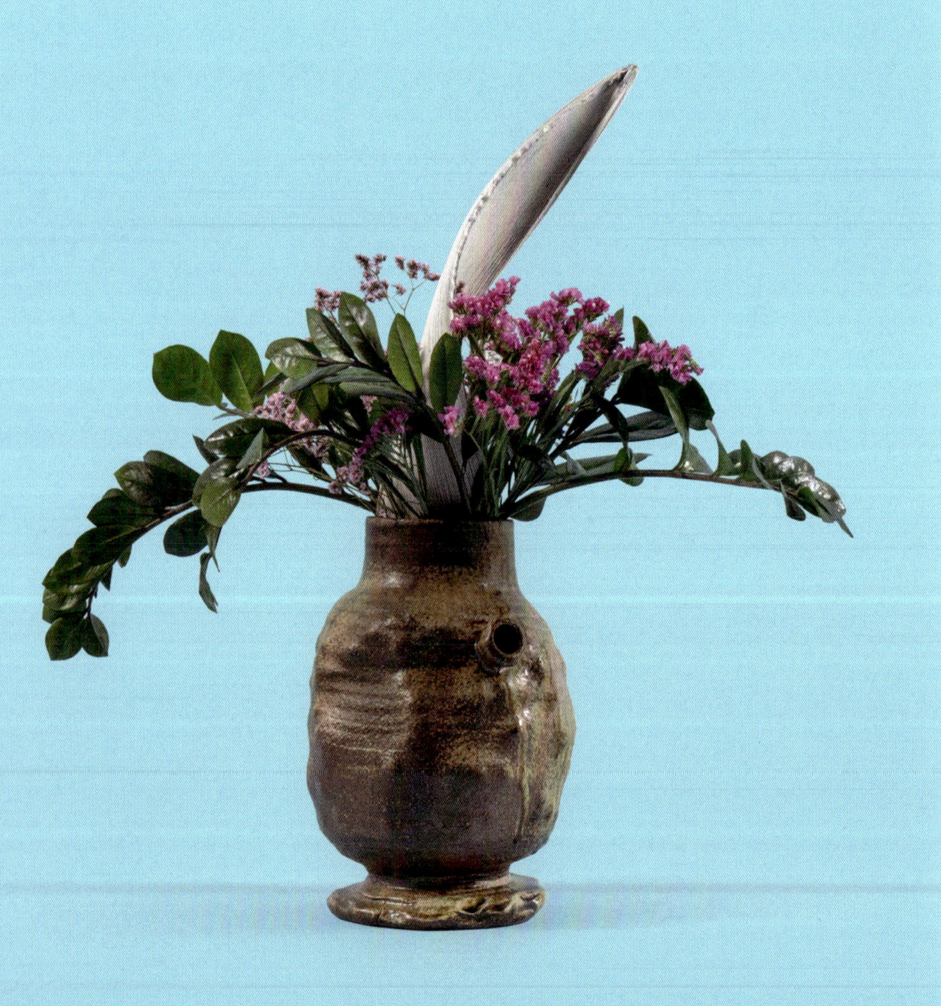

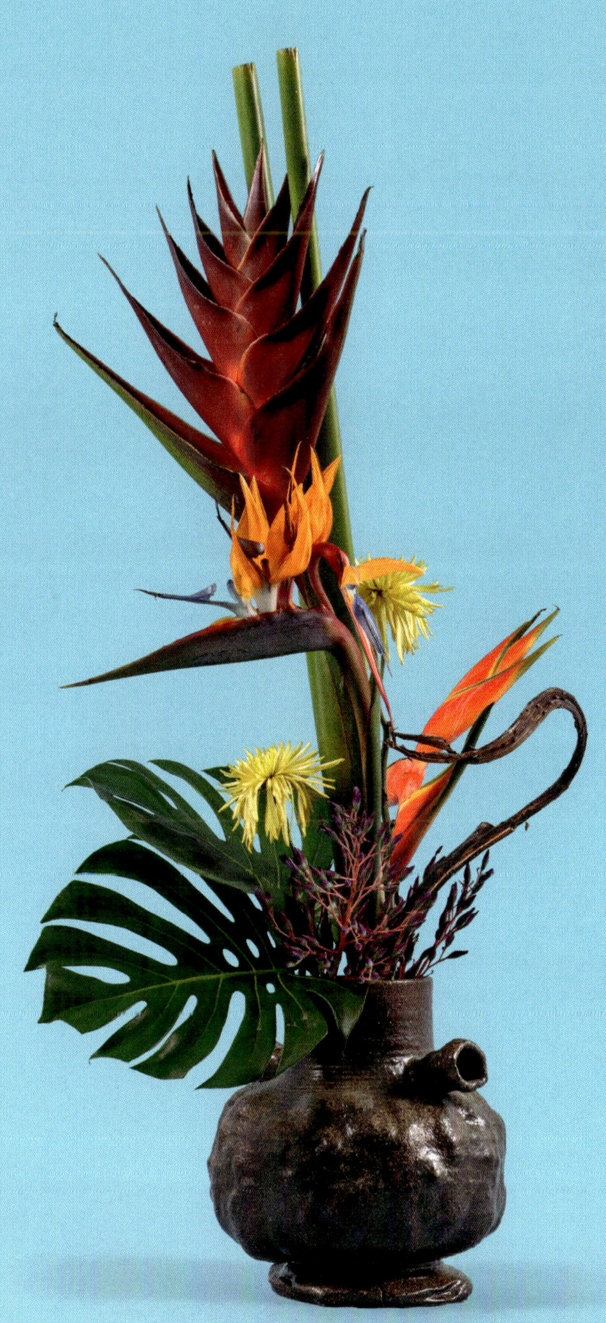

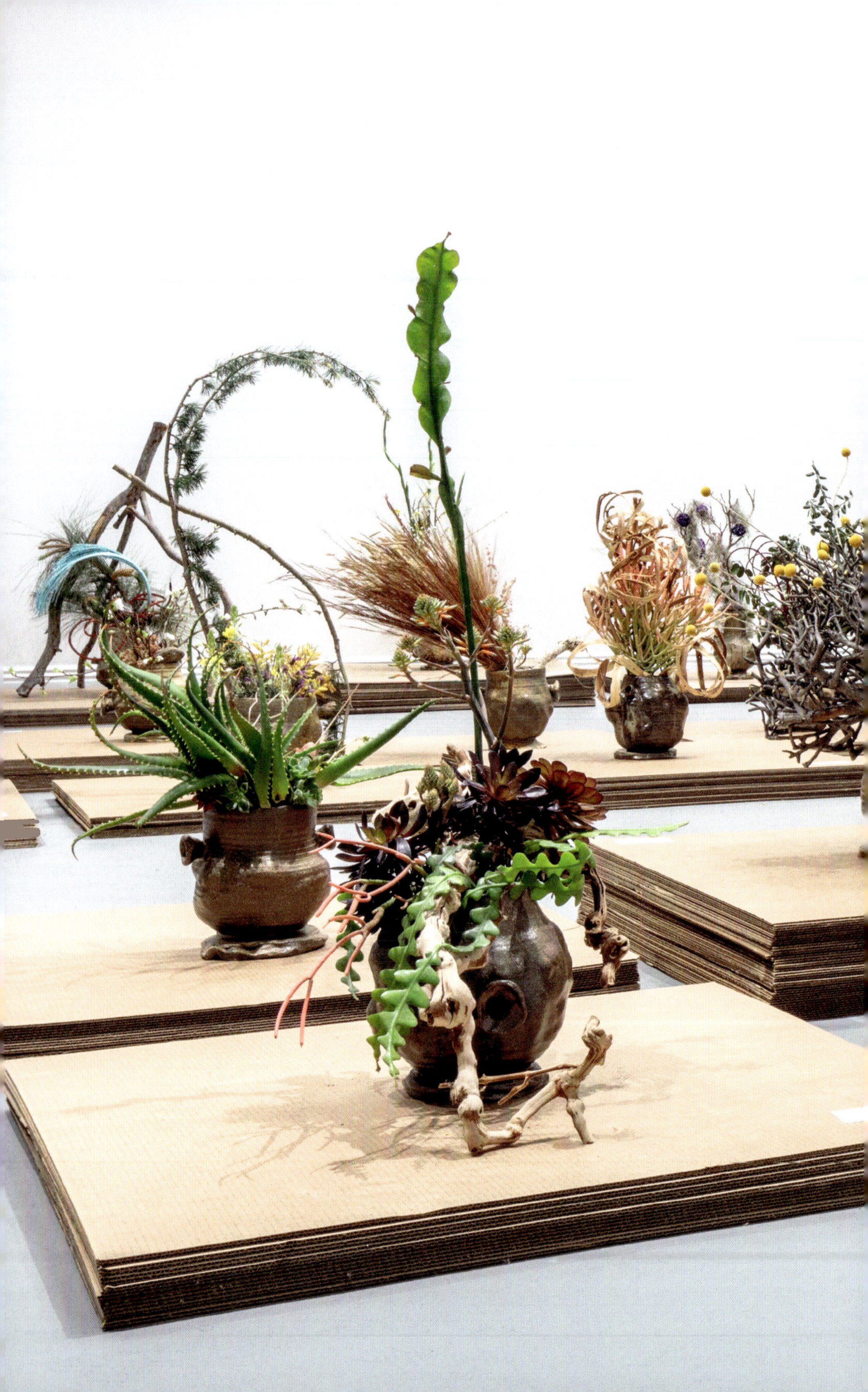

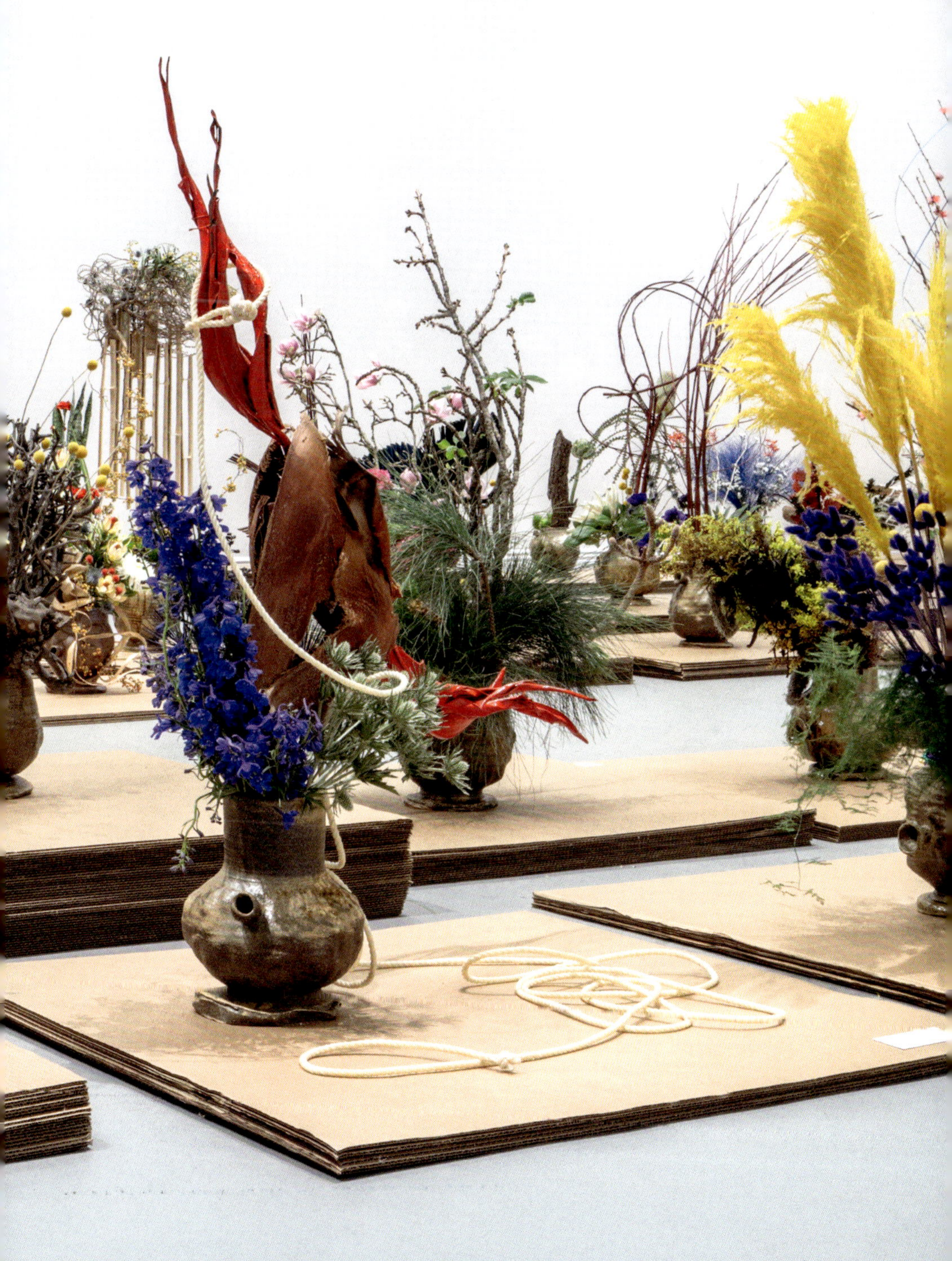

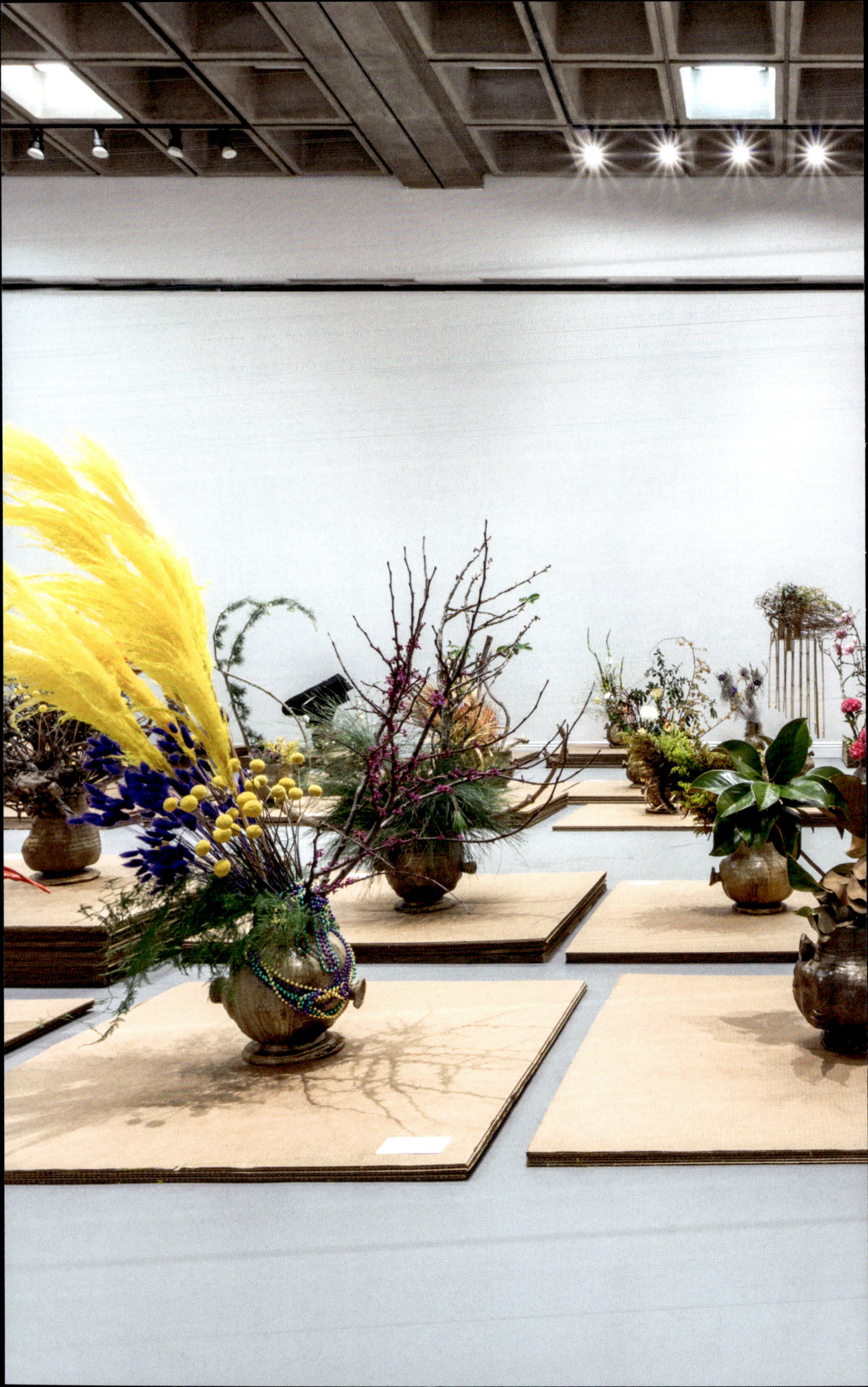

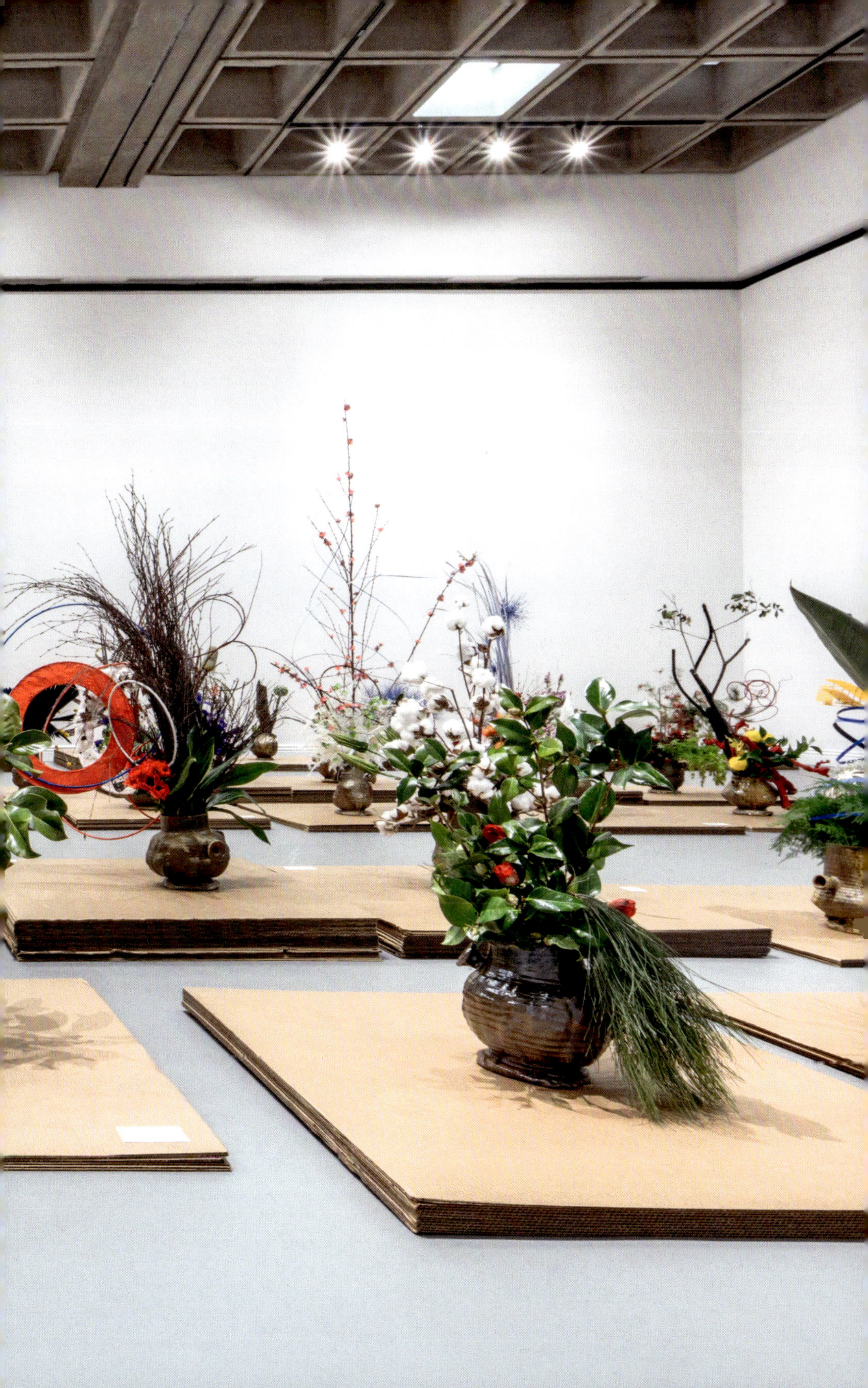

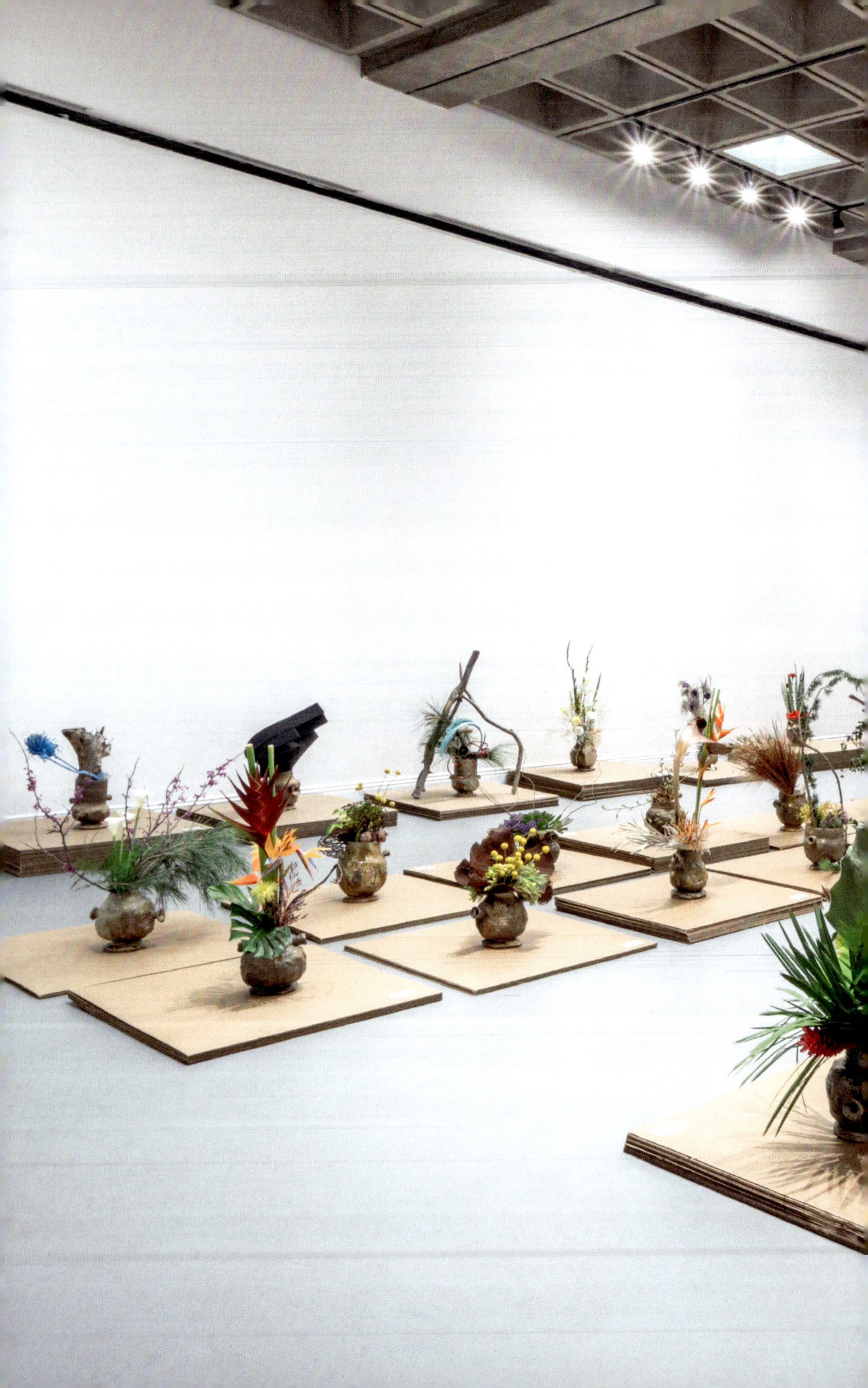

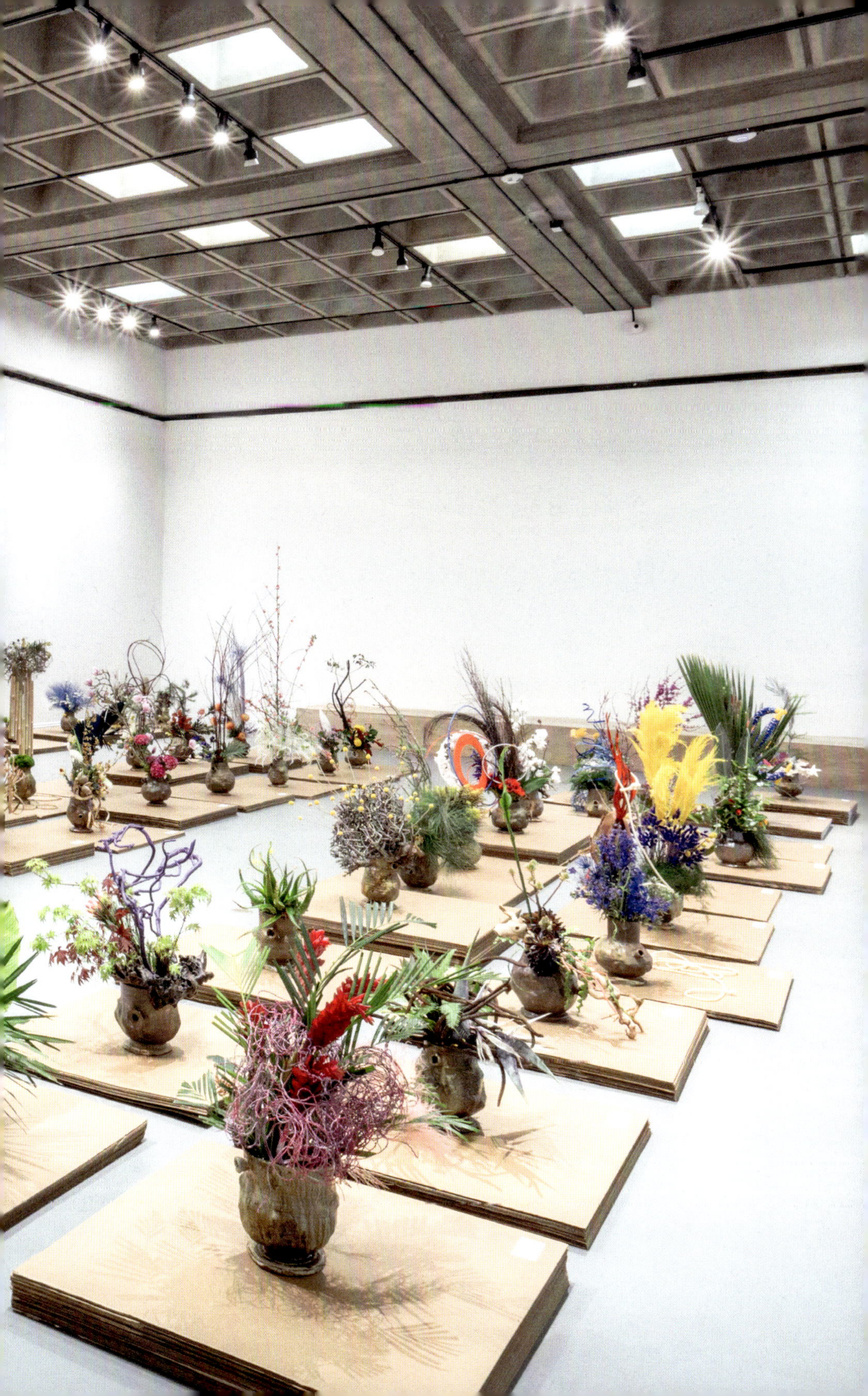

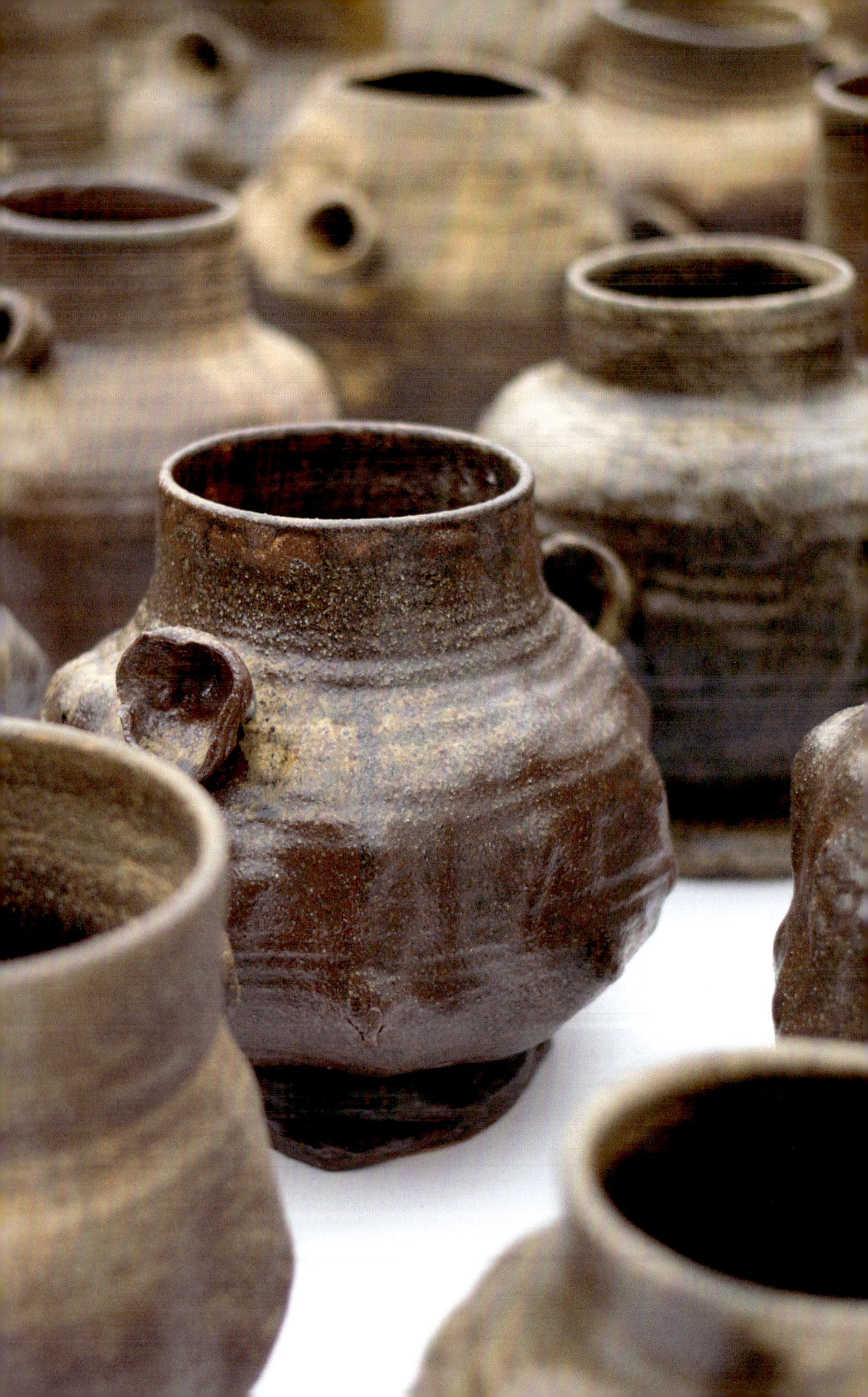

COMMON GROUND

ADAM SILVERMAN

In fall 2019 I began a project to address the political and cultural divisions in the United States.

Before there was America the country, or the individual states and the ensuing territorial identities and resulting politics, there was the land that America occupies. If you picture what the country (or the entire planet) looks like from space, it is brown (the ground: clay), blue (the oceans, lakes, rivers: water), and green (the plants and trees: wood ash).

This project, *Common Ground*, involves gathering those three foundational materials from each of the fifty states plus Washington DC and the five inhabited US territories (Puerto Rico, the US Virgin Islands, Guam, American Samoa, and the Northern Mariana Islands). The materials were mixed together, erasing the arbitrary borders of statehood, to create a single new, unique composite that became the heart of this project. The origin materials were treated with the reverence and stewardship they are entitled to and with respect for all that they contain and represent. *Common Ground* reflects on the divisiveness of the current state of the country while also celebrating the commonality and universality of the shared American and human experience.

There are two parts to this project. One is a set of fifty-six plates, fifty-six bowls, and fifty-six cups. The second is a group of fifty-six ceremonial pots.

Preceding pages: Ceremonial vessels and ikebana works displayed at George J. Doizaki Gallery, Japanese American Cultural & Community Center, Los Angeles, CA, 2022.

All the pieces physically embody the combined earth, trees, and water from each state and territory. The forms of these ceremonial pots are not subtle. Although they stand on strong feet or foundations, they are battered, scarred, leaning over—showing the processes that got them here. The tops are open, symbolically ready to receive and hold new ideas, feelings, conversations, and objects. They have handles that are reminiscent of ears. They share a formal language with pots from most stages in history and most geographies, both functional and ritualistic (urns, chalices, amphorae, trophies, storage jars). In the end, all the pieces have an identical material DNA, and each group of pieces comprises the same form, yet they all have very distinct individual characteristics. They share more similarities than differences.

My hope is that this project will bring people together in collaboration and community and create opportunities for dialogue and bridge-building; that it will, in both a very literal and material way, and a symbolic and abstract way, show the richness that results when celebrating the diversity and commonality of America, its origins, its culture(s), and all the people who live here.

This catalogue presents the results of a collaboration with Sogetsu Ikebana, Los Angeles, focusing on the fifty-six ceremonial pots.

Determining what forms to make for this project was challenging. The process began with making sketches of what the pots could be. For the last fifteen to twenty years I have made hundreds of different versions of eggs and spheres, many of them mounted on some type of pedestal. There was an appeal to making a "pure" form, especially one that references birth or rebirth.

However, it felt like some simple gestures toward the intent of the project made more sense. The form should be open rather than closed. It should stand on a strong foot, have handles that reference ears. It should be battered and bruised in a way that reflects its creation and its status as a material ambassador of this land.

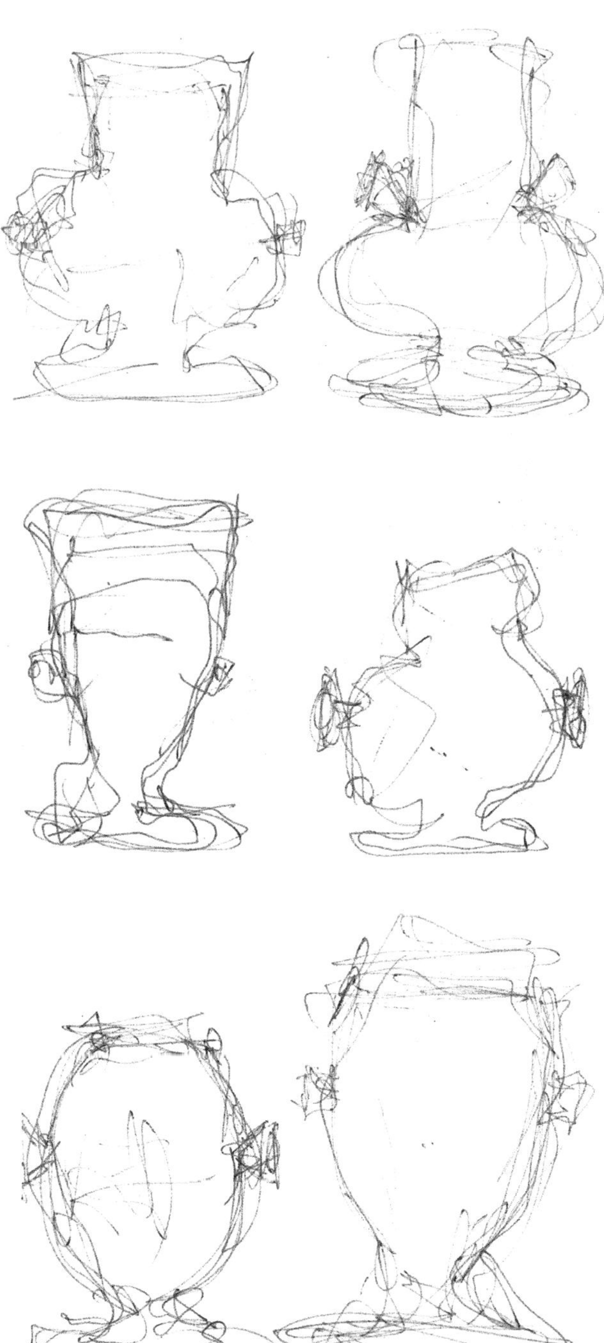

The materials were collected with the help of a vast community of people who came together spontaneously around this project.

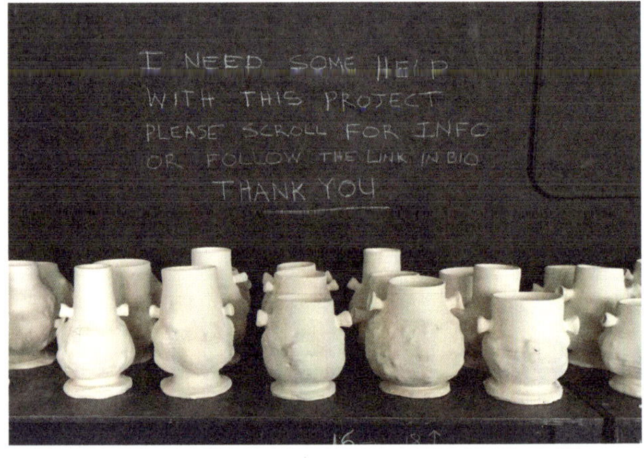

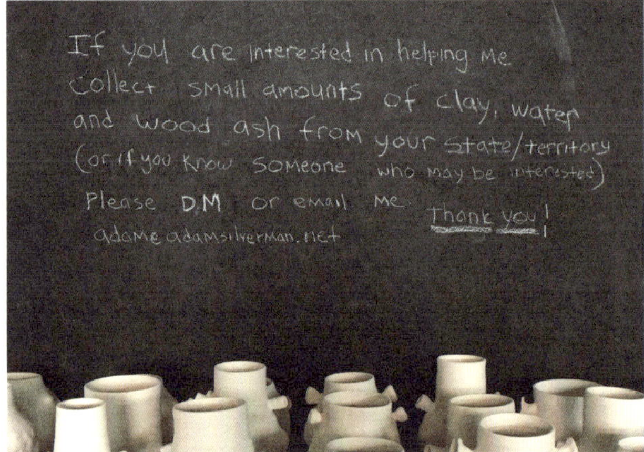

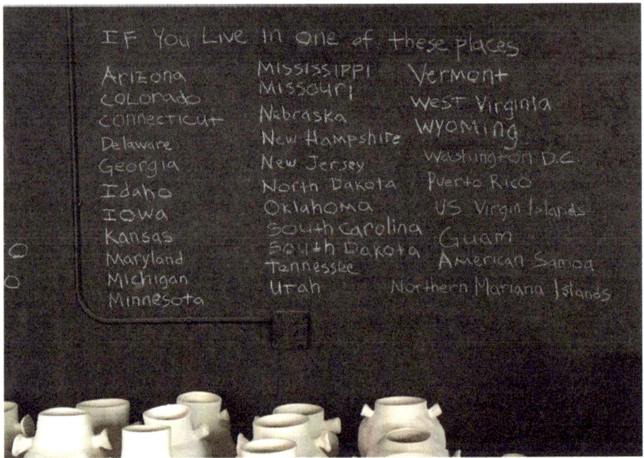

Each person who was interested in collecting clay, wood ash, and water was sent a USPS Priority Mail box a strong water bottle, two one-gallon heavy duty bags (one for clay and one for wood ash), and a piece of paper with a few questions about the sources of the materials.

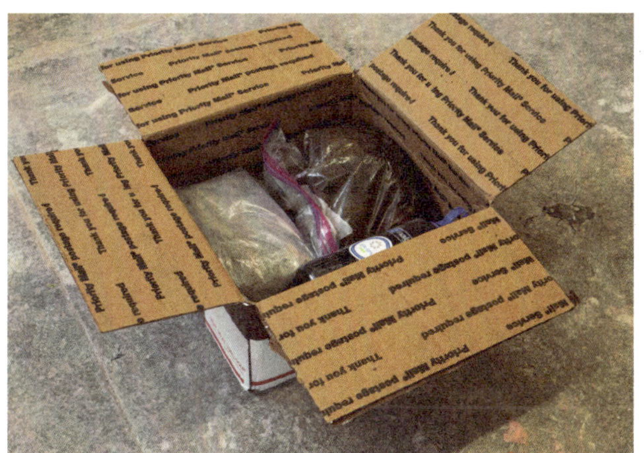

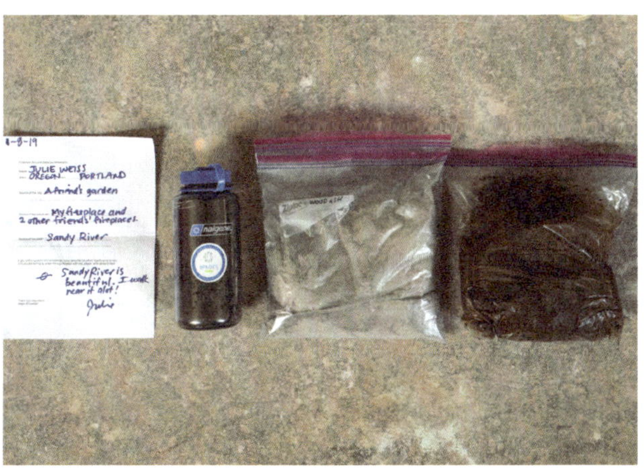

Once the materials arrived at my studio, the water was transferred to glass bottles and stored until I had everything from all fifty-six states and territories (which took over a year).

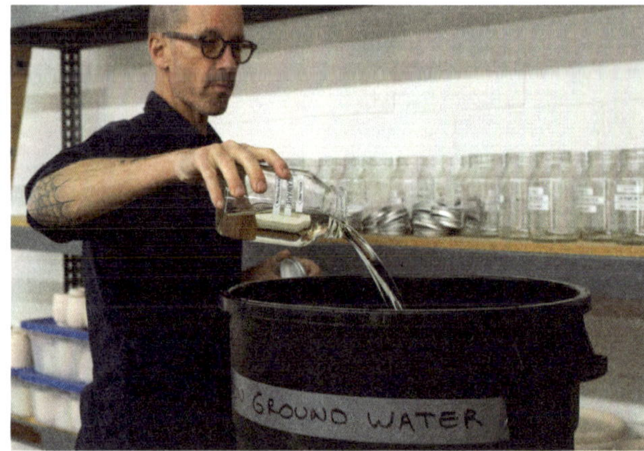

Here, the fifty-six water samples from taps, wells, fountains, streams, rivers, lakes, oceans—and even melted snow from Maine—are being combined to comprise a single body of water.

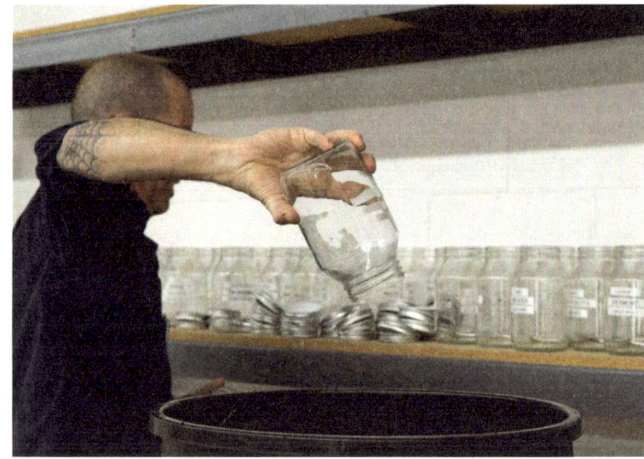

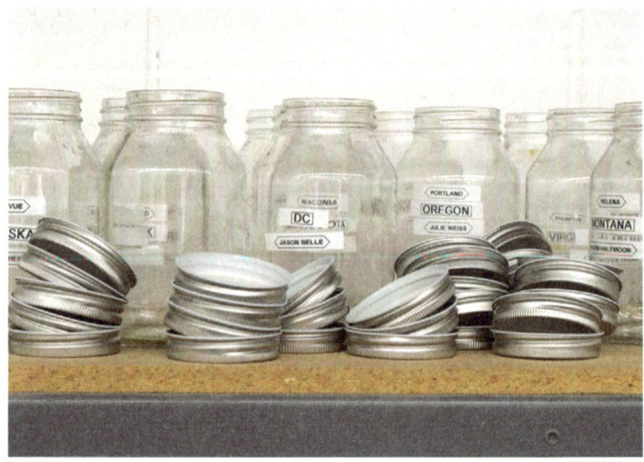

The fifty-six wood ash samples being combined into a single material.

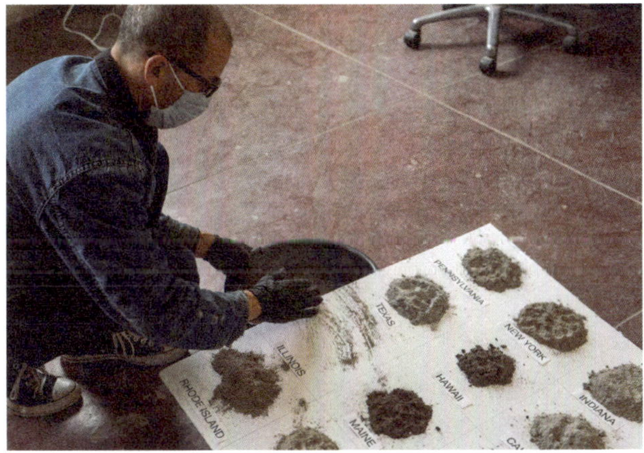

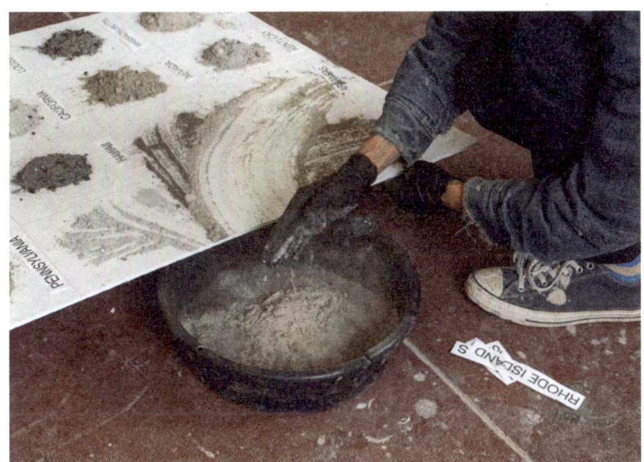

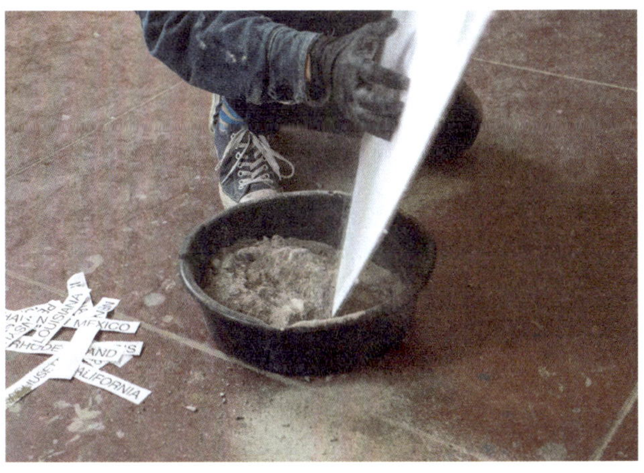

Before combining, the ash was pushed through screens to remove nails, rocks, wood chunks, and other debris found in fires.

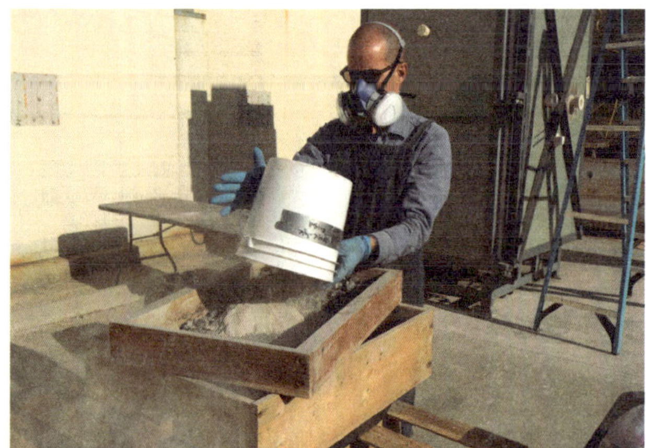

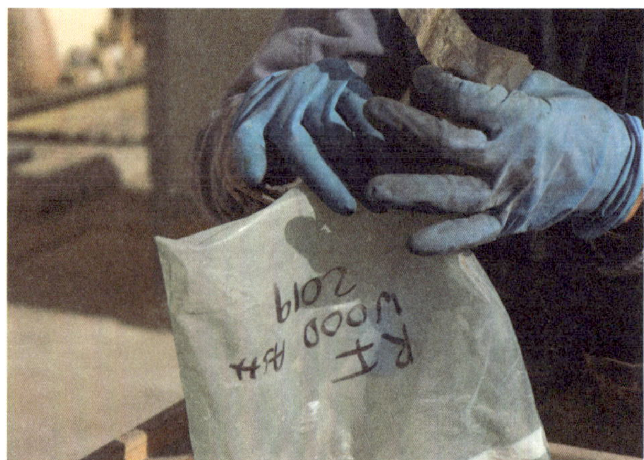

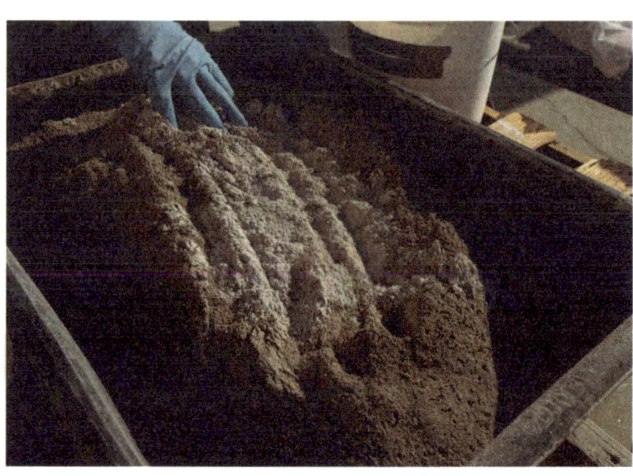

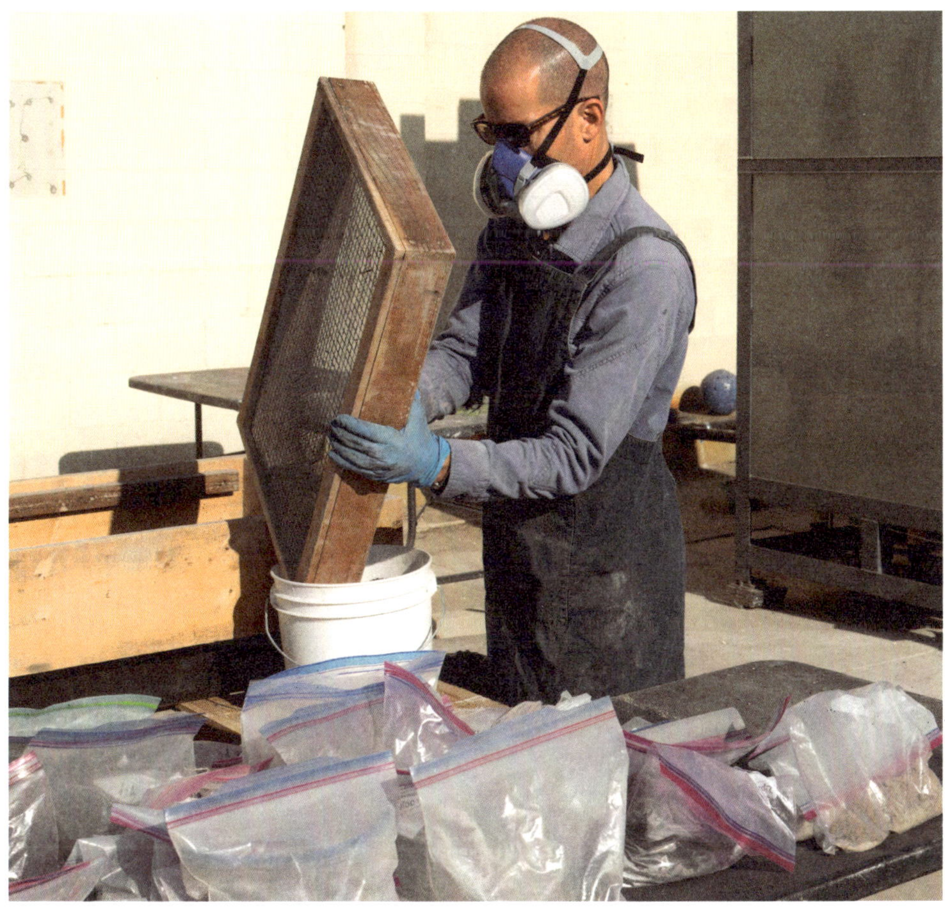

The colors, textures, tastes, and smells of the ashes from the different states and territories reflect the amazing diversity of this country.

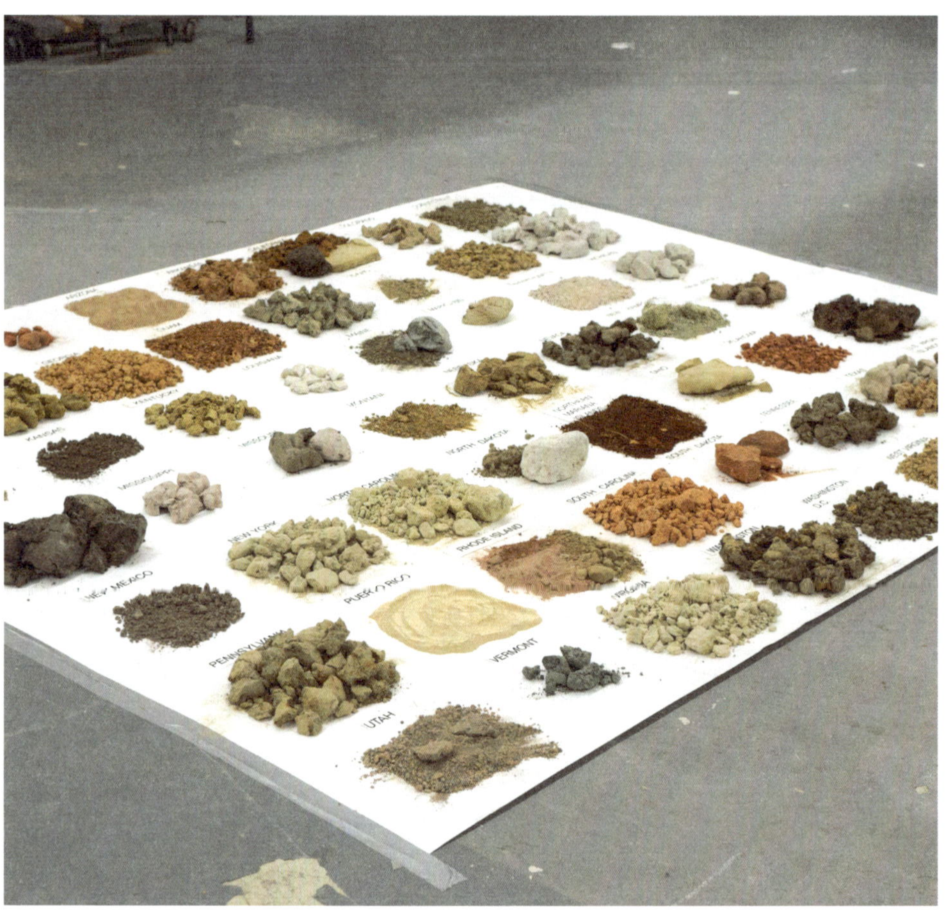

After all the clays arrived at my studio, I laid them out in a twelve-by-twelve-inch grid on white paper so that we could take a birds-eye photograph of everything together before it was mixed into a single clay compound.

Once we had the pictures, I said goodbye to each individual clay sample and swept them into a large mixing bucket.

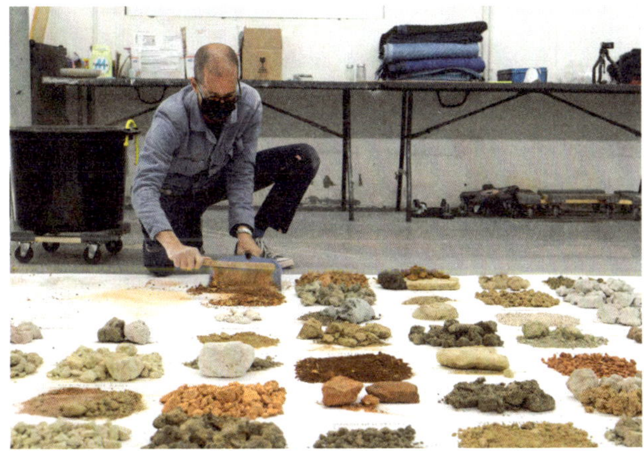

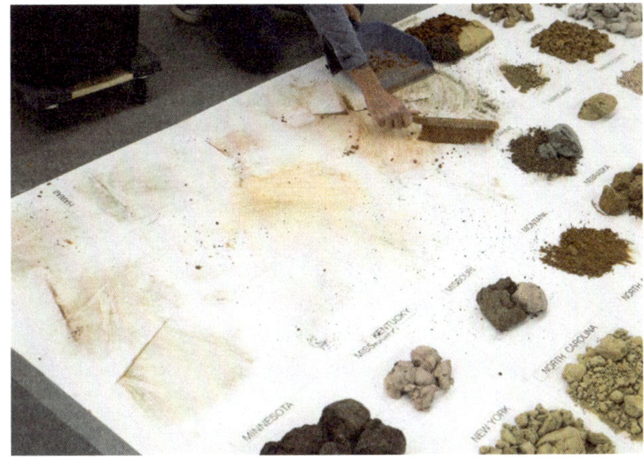

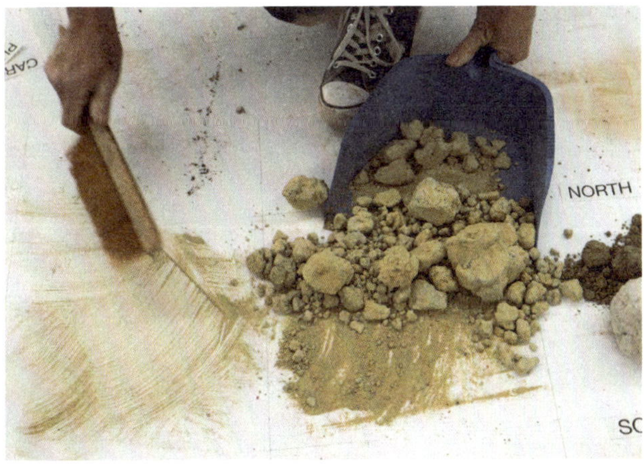

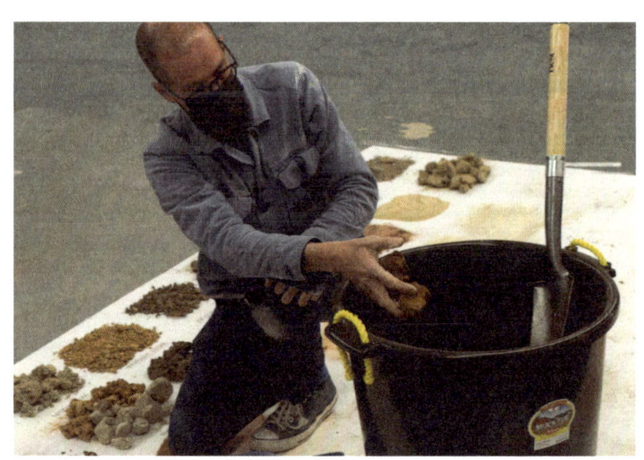

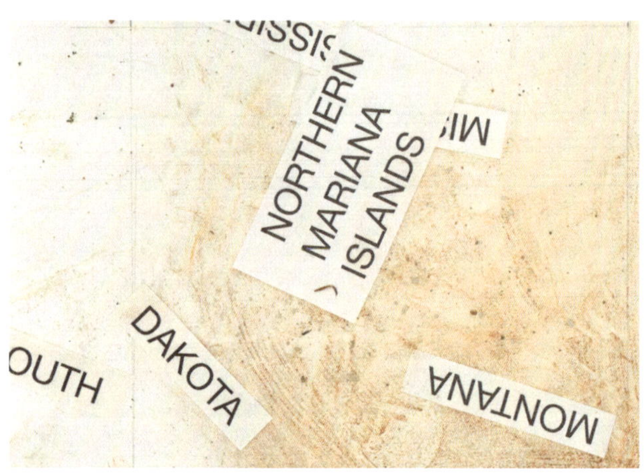
NORTHERN
MARIANA
ISLANDS
DAKOTA
MONTANA

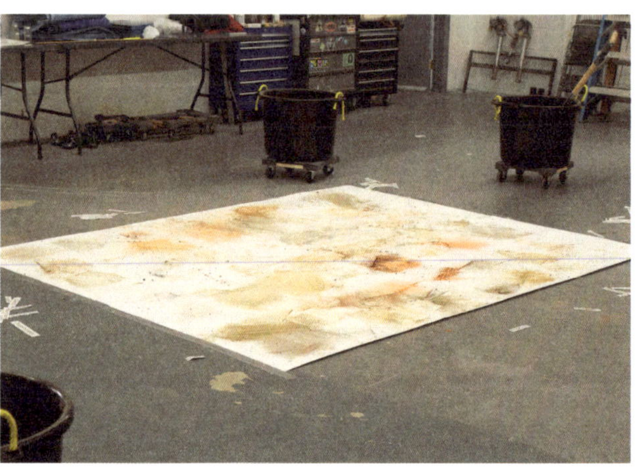

The first step in integrating the fifty-six clays into one, united clay body is soaking it all in large tubs of water.

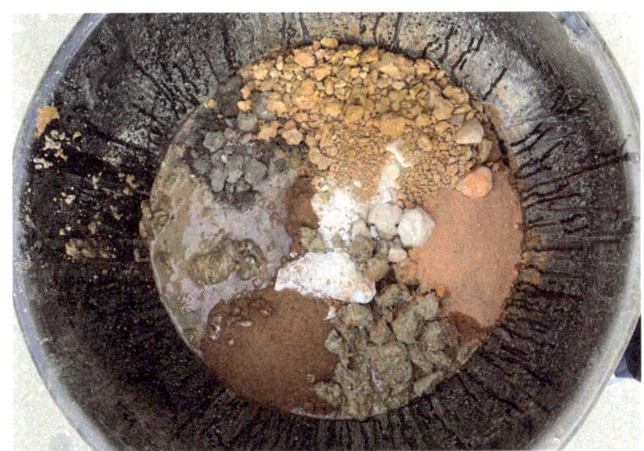

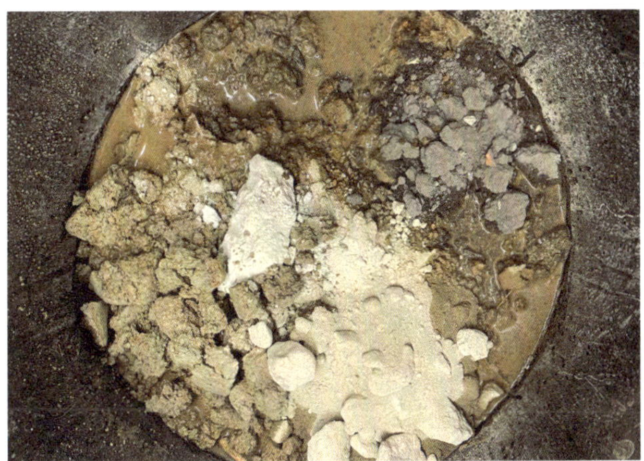

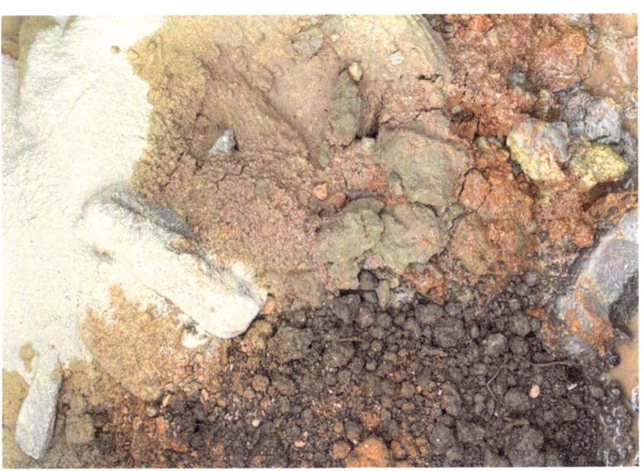

Processing the clays is slow and laborious. From the soaking tubs, the wet mix is then pushed through a series of screens, with decreasingly smaller openings to remove rocks and impurities.

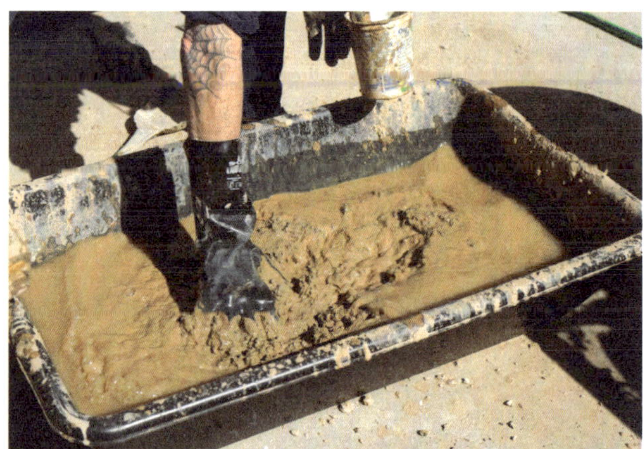

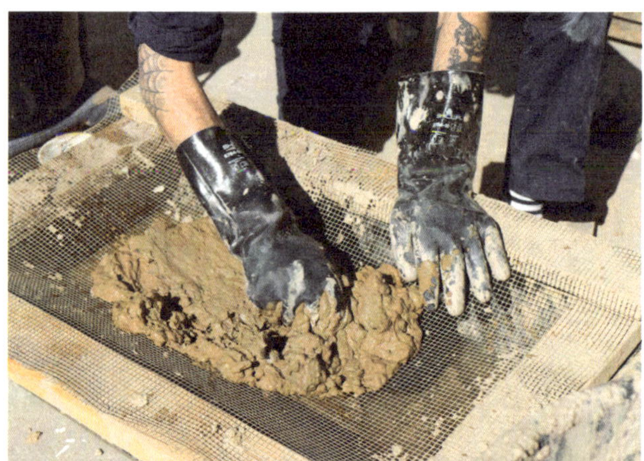

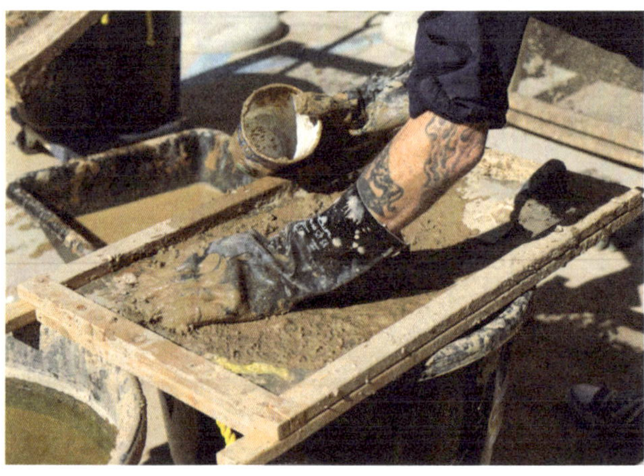

The clean clay is then laid out on large canvas slings where it dries into sheets that are a half-inch to one-inch thick. Those are then broken into pieces, put into large tubs, and crushed with a sledgehammer. It is then made into smaller batches and pulverized using a mortar and pestle.

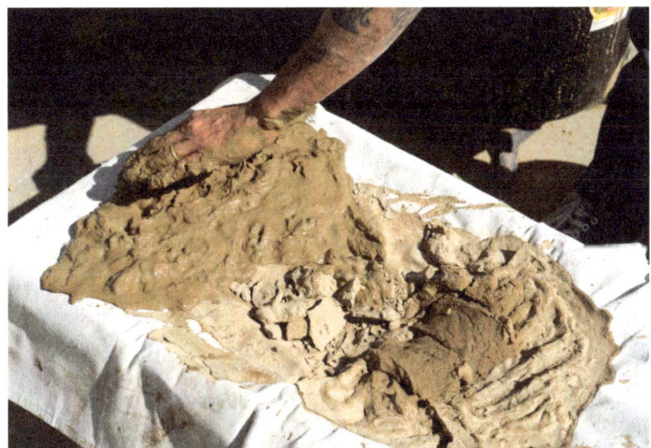

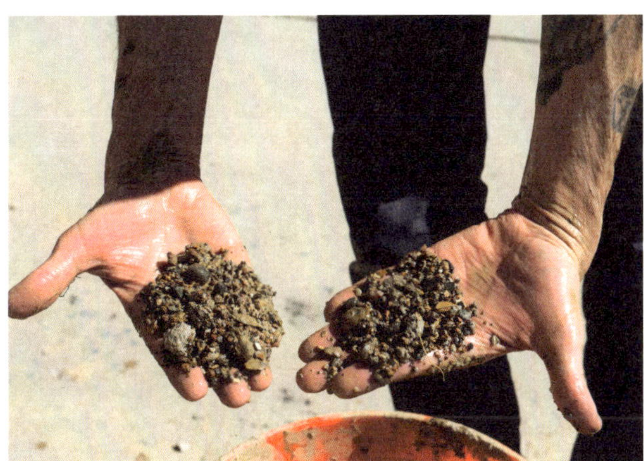

The final powdered clay is then mixed again to ensure that all the fifty-six different clays are fully integrated into a single new clay.

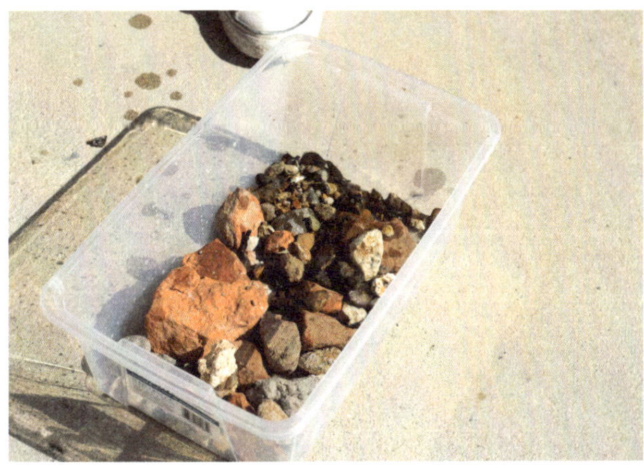

Testing and firing small batches of glazes made from different ratios of clay, ash, and water mixed together.

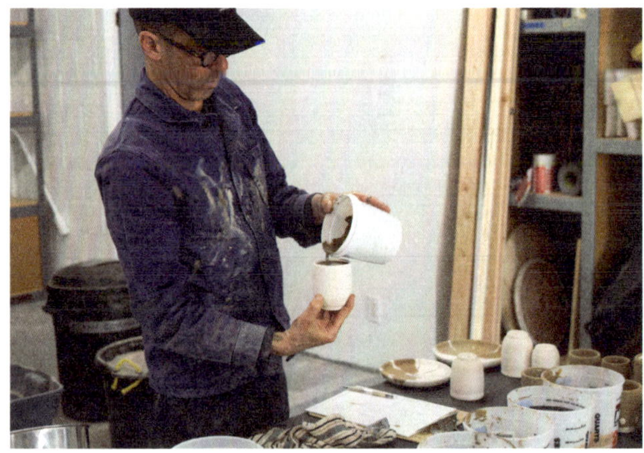

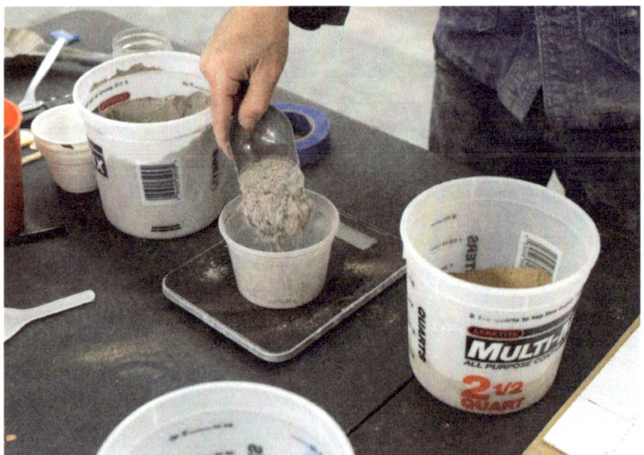

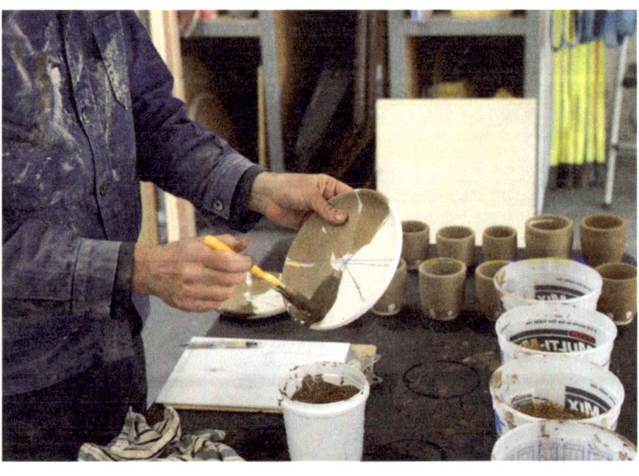

Firing a bunch of test pieces in different kilns at different temperatures and in different environments to see what these materials can do and what they could become.

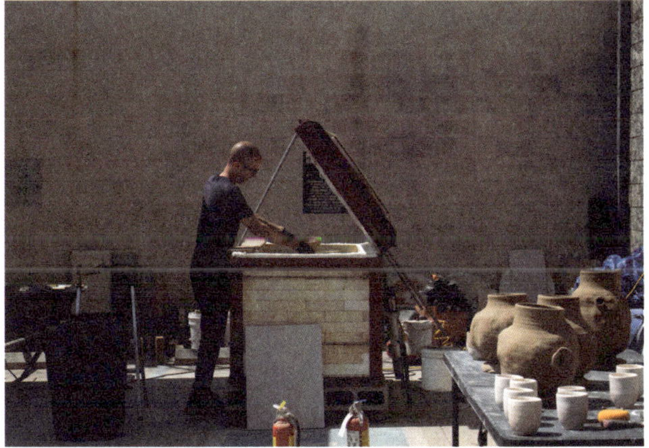

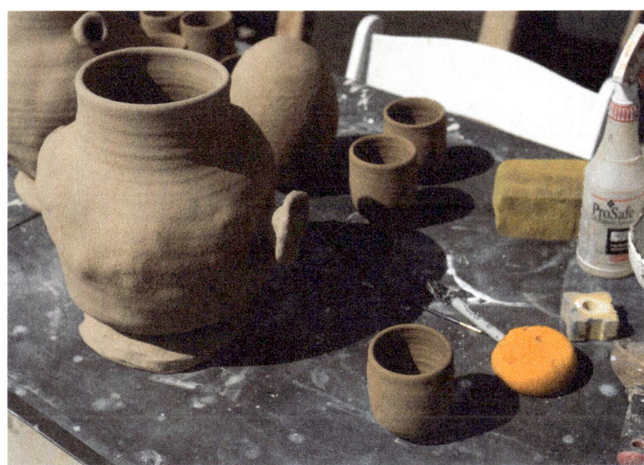

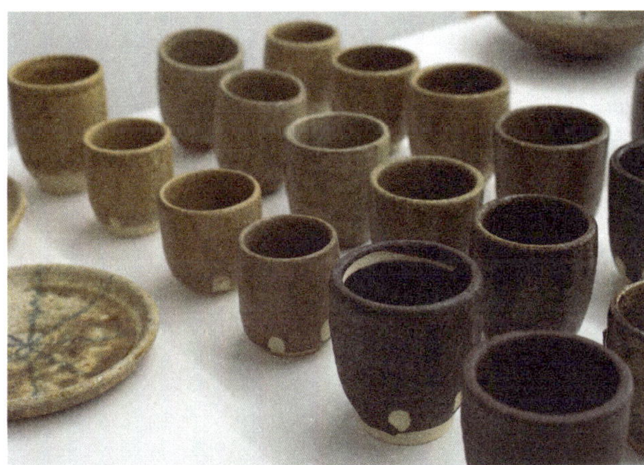

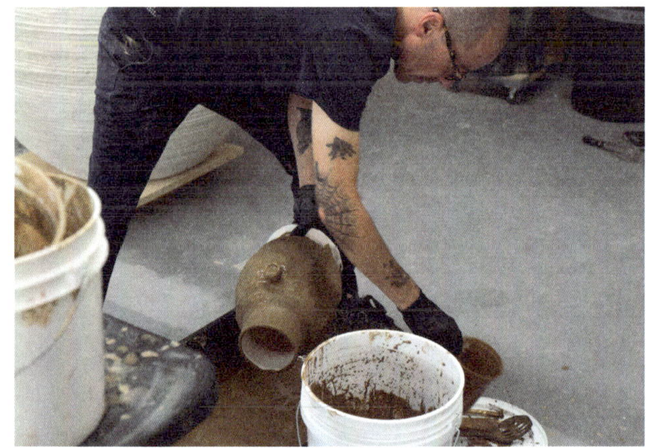

Glazing the final pots with the final glaze recipe of 90 percent clay, 10 percent ash, plus water.

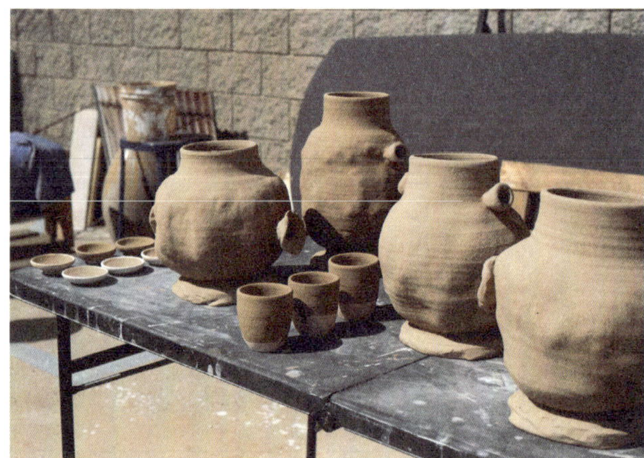

Glazed pieces ready for firing.

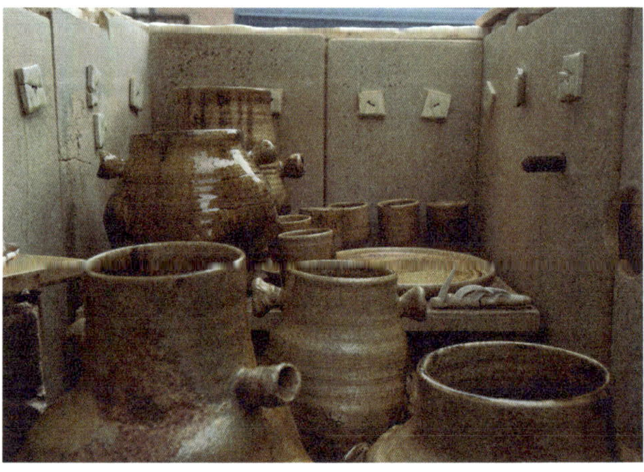

Cooling kiln, post-firing. This kiln typically ranges from about cone 12 in the front to cone 10 in the rear. The visible cone pack shows cones 9,10, and 11 down and 12 softening and is about 2/3 of the way back in the kiln.

Unloading the kiln.

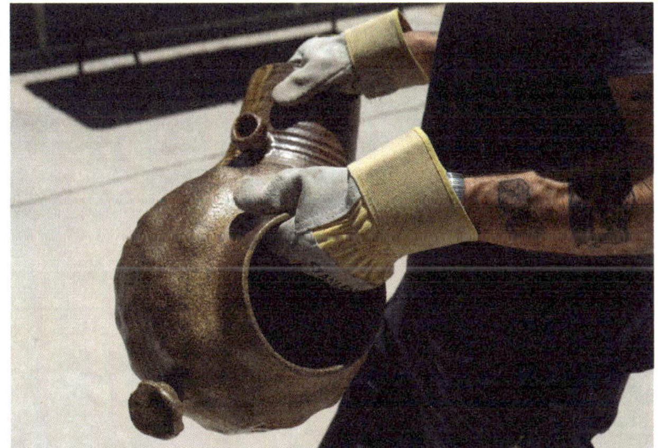

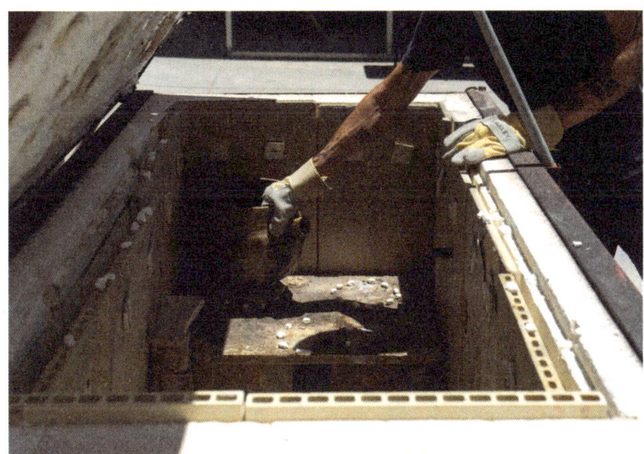

Finished *Common Ground* ceremonial pots slowly assembled on this big table as they were completed over the course of about a year.

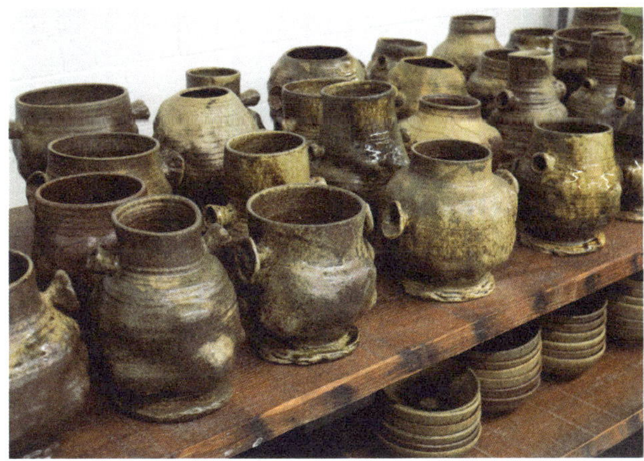

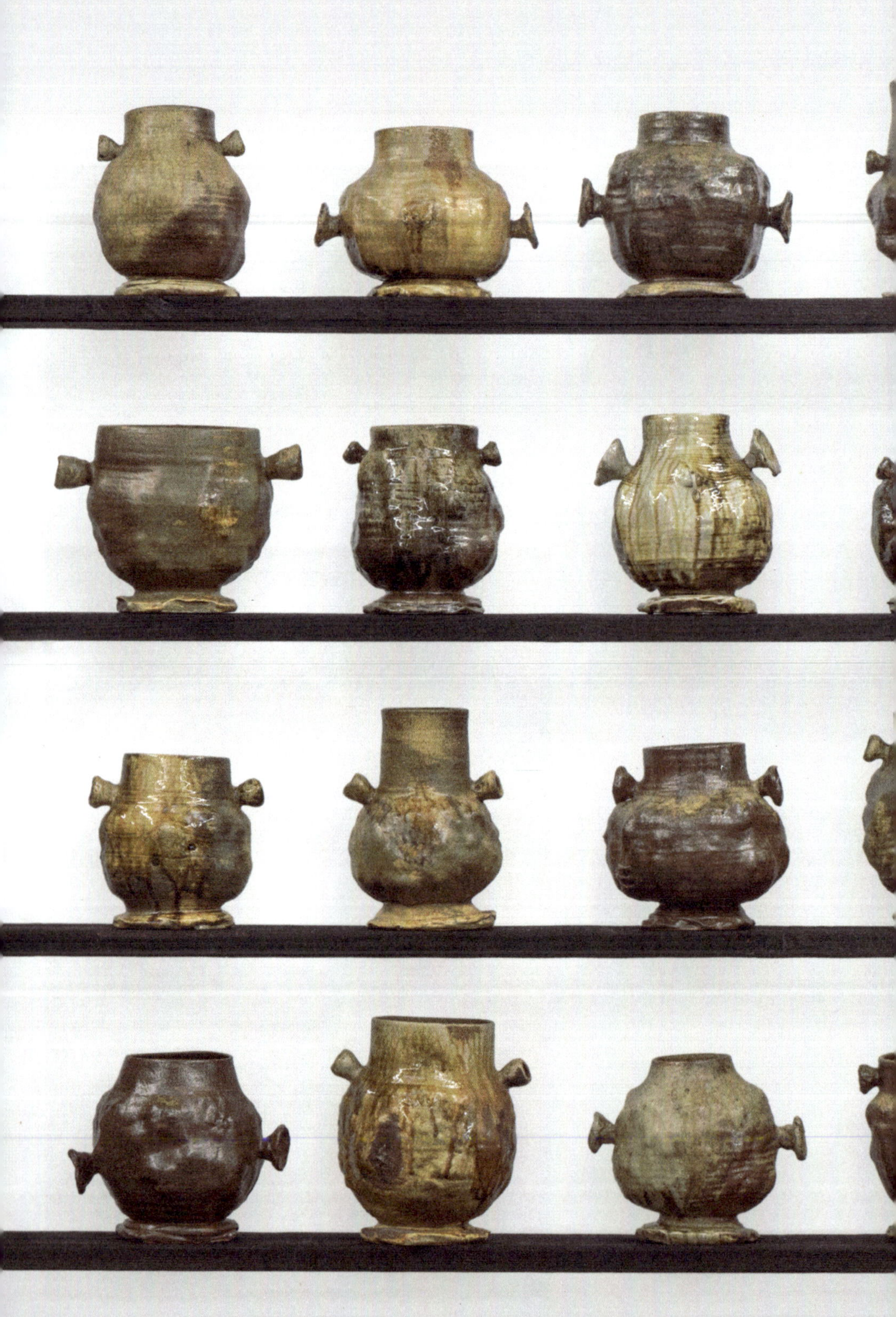

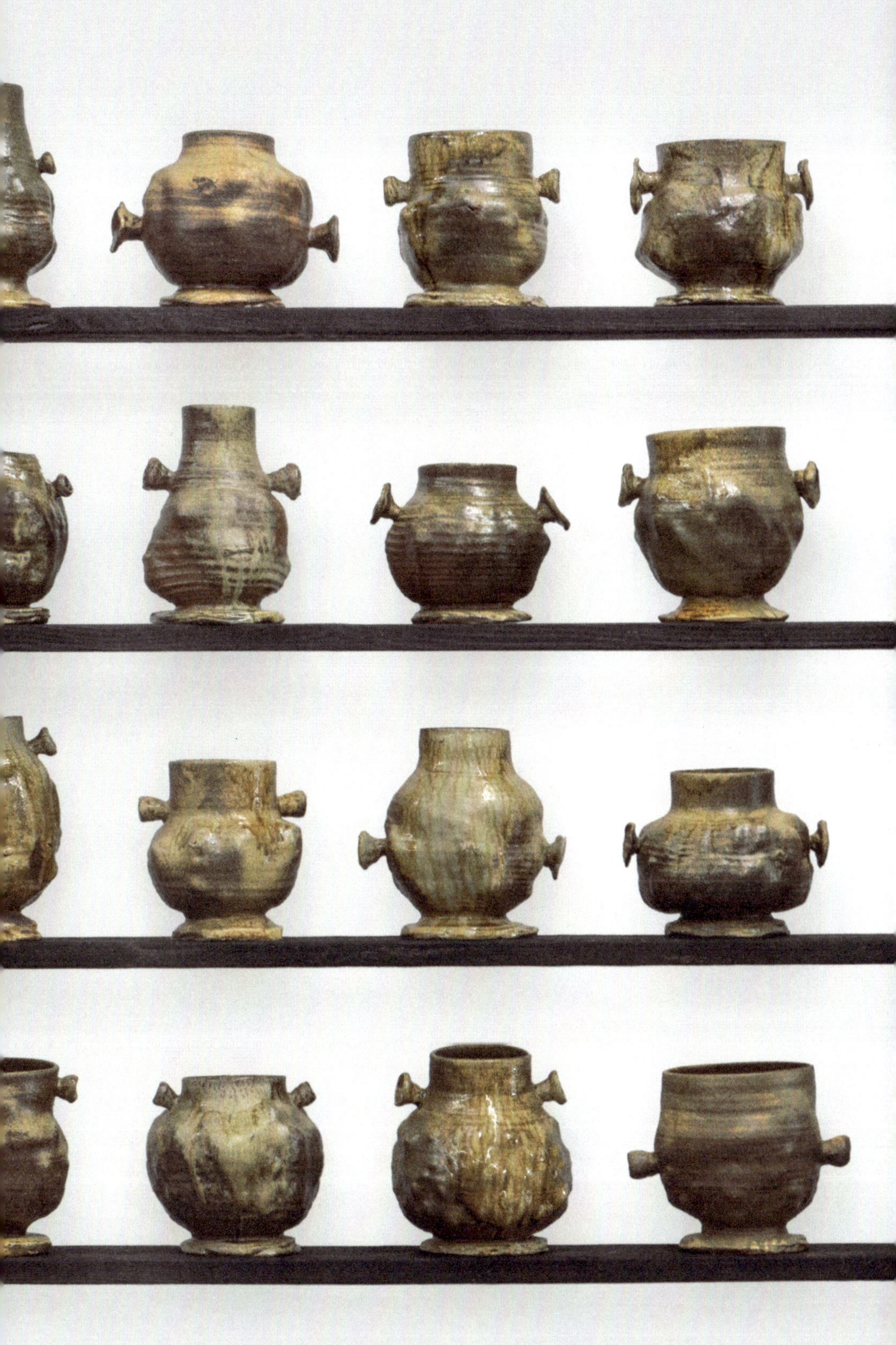

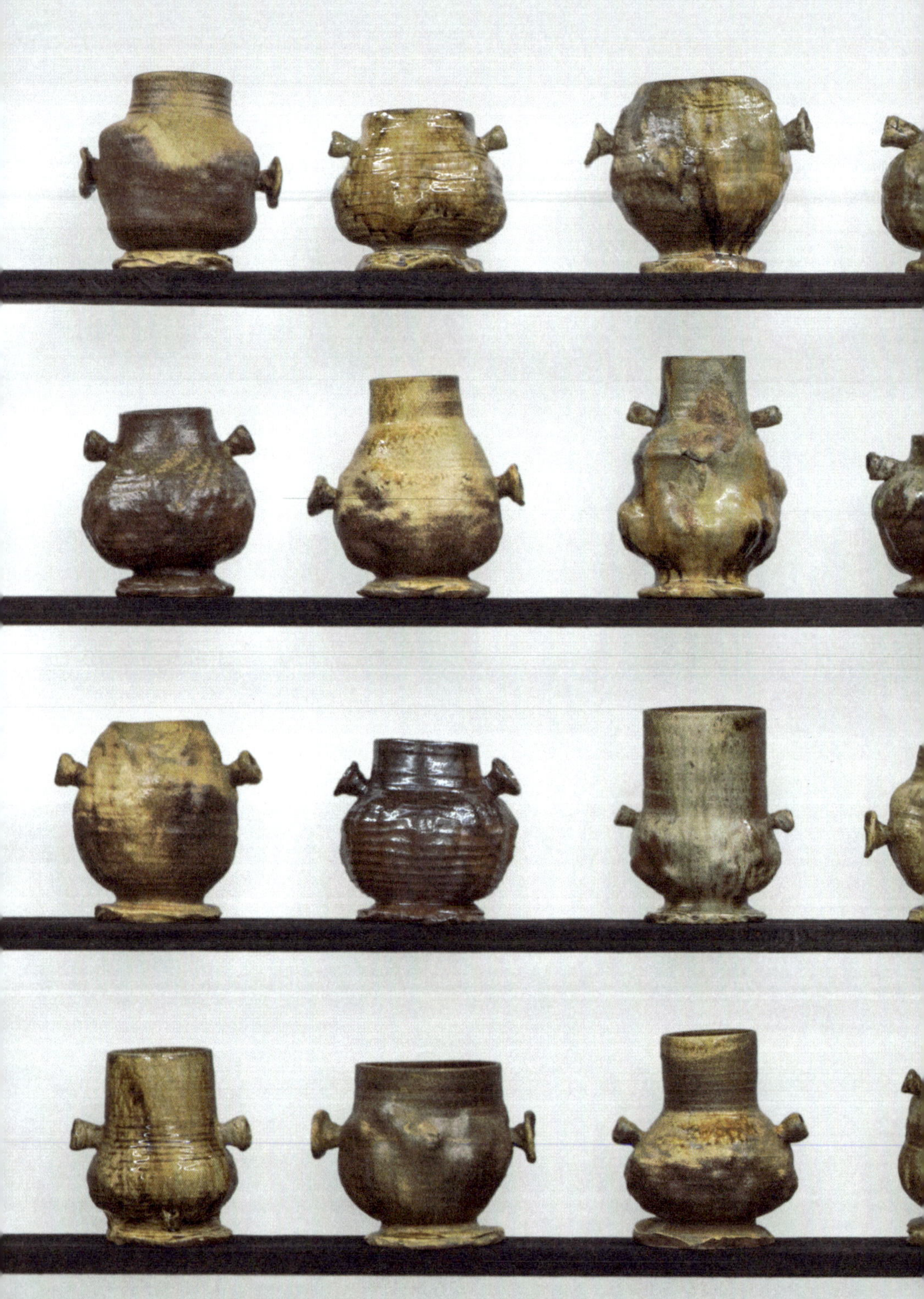

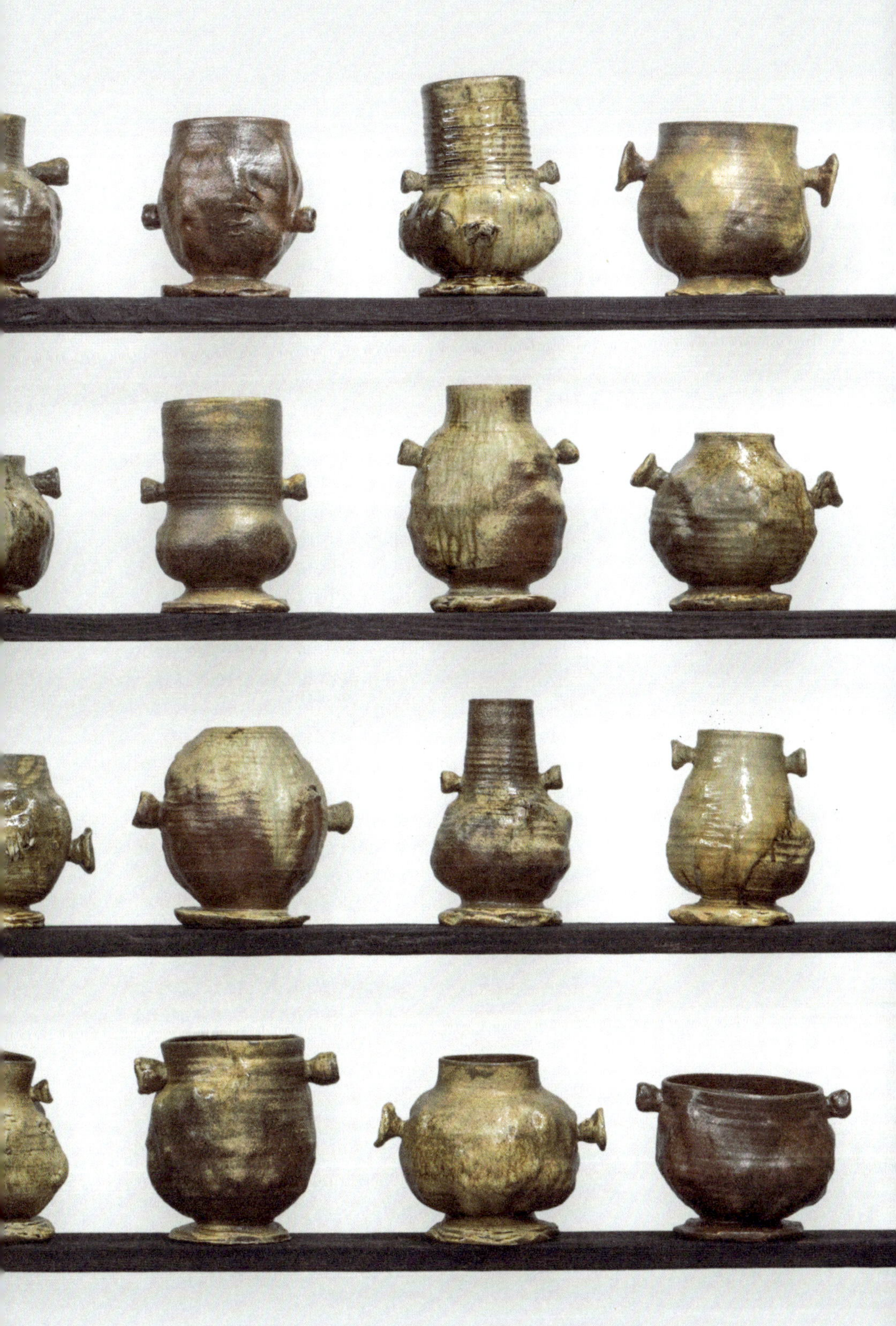

ART OF THE GROUND

RAVI GUNEWARDENA

When Adam Silverman contacted me about collaborating with him on the *Common Ground* project in 2021, the idea of placing ikebana in his earthen pots immediately provoked some exhilarating possibilities. The relationship between the vessel and plants is a deeply connected one in ikebana, with the form of the vessel and its openings informing the composition of the arrangement. The material (ceramic, porcelain, bamboo, metal) and heft of a vessel can influence the selection of plants by the ikebana artist. For centuries, the shapes of vases were prescribed, along with the ikebana works to be placed within them. Early guidebooks, such as *Kaō irai no Kadensho,* a late fifteenth-century chronicle of ikebana by the masters in the Ikenobo school, depicted arrangements of varying complexity which served as examples to be followed by ikebana students for centuries to come.

The shapes of vessels were given specific names: tall vertical vases are called *nageire,* meaning "thrown in," shallow tray-shaped containers are known as *moribana,* "heaped up flowers," and rounded vases with wide openings are named *tsubo,* or "pot." Seasoned ikebana masters and students develop the skills of responding to the shape of the vessel with their work. Yet if several ikebana artists were given vessels of the same shape and the same plant material to create an arrangement, the resulting works would vary greatly.

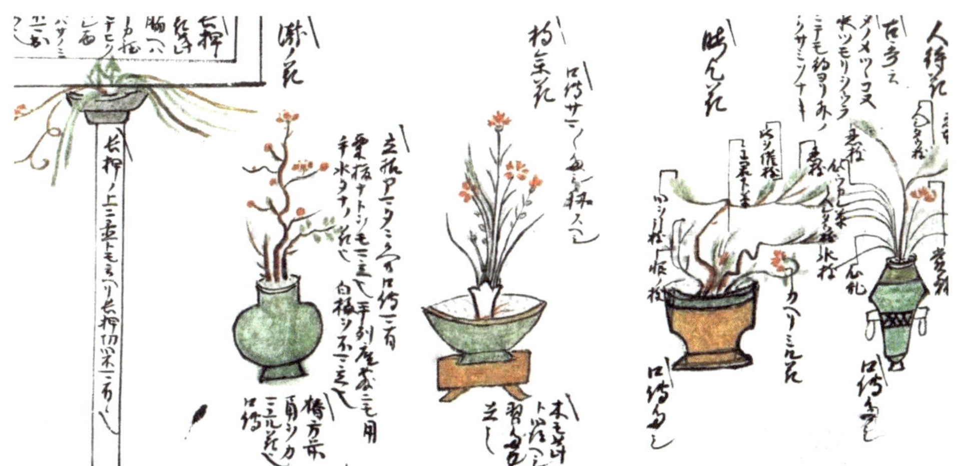

From *Kaō irai no Kadensho*—late fifteenth-century chronicle of ikebana arrangements by Ikenobo masters.

With this knowledge at hand, the discussion with Adam continued further, considering the participation by the entire membership of the Sogetsu Ikebana Los Angeles branch and the broad range of responses such a collaboration could yield. While the fifty-six vessels were essentially the same shape, a hybrid of *nageire* and *tsubo* shapes with biomorphic ear-like attachments, there was still a fair amount of variation within the collection. Since the vessels were composed of material from fifty-six locations, we discussed whether or not to conjure an aspect of place in each arrangement.

Among the classical types of ikebana arrangements is the Rikka style—a seven, nine, or eleven-branched assembly symbolizing the Buddhist cosmology of Mount Meru; a layering of realms representing the universe. Various branches can represent geographical features such as peak, waterfall, hill, valley, or town, separated into sun and shade. Simplified three-element *shōka* arrangements embody heaven, earth, and man (in Japanese: *shin*, *soe*, and *hikae* in the Sogetsu school tradition). So, if an ikebana work can symbolize the embodiment of the cosmos,

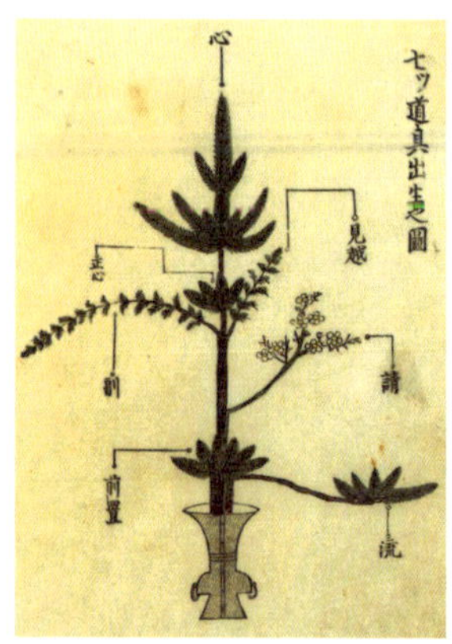

Rikka arrangement diagram, from the book *Rikka Shodo Shu* by Jinkyusai, 1684.

the idea of representing a state or territory in an arrangement presented a credible concept for this exhibition.

In addition to the various traditional types of arrangements mentioned earlier, developments in the Sogetsu school, founded in 1927 by Sofu Teshigahara, made possible a new type—*zen'ei* ikebana, or avant-garde flower arranging—which questioned the established rules, manipulated plants in new ways, and even incorporated non-plant materials such as metal, glass, and plastic. This experimental attitude pervades the work of Sogetsu practitioners in different ways.

As the exhibition neared, each of the Sogetsu Los Angeles participants were assigned a vase with a state to represent. The interpretations of how to represent a state or territory were left to the participants, resulting in an interesting array of responses. Some artists chose to represent a cultural aspect associated with the location, some chose geographically associated plants, and others made more obscure references.

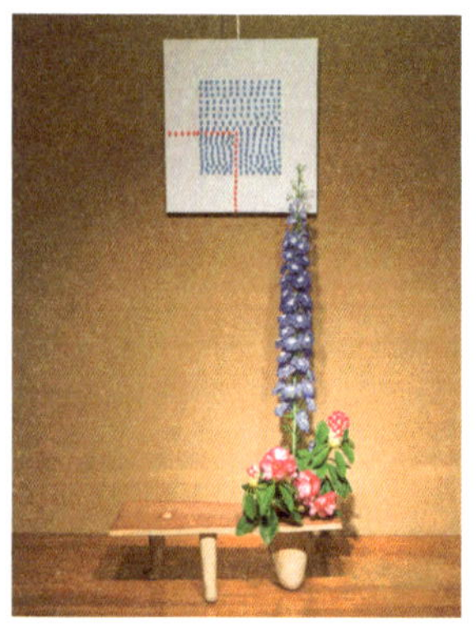

Isamu Noguchi, *Sansoku hanaike* (Three-legged vase), 1952, Shigaraki stoneware, used in an ikebana arrangement. Installation view, Sogetsu 90th anniversary exhibition, *Complementing an Artwork*, Tokyo, April 2017. Painting by artist Kishio Suga.

The Los Angeles branch of Sogetsu was established in 1985 as one of several new outposts of the Tokyo-based school. While a few ikebana senseis (teachers) from Japan had been spreading the teachings individually since the postwar period through a multischool organization called Ikebana International, local branches of Sogetsu were only formally recognized by the parent institution in more recent decades. The making of vessels and collaborating with ceramic artists has remained an important aspect of the practice of ikebana both in Japan and chapters abroad. In Los Angeles, a select group of senseis and students make their own ceramic vessels. Works by Kaz Yokou Kitajima and Masuo Ojima are collected by and featured in works by several Sogetsu Los Angeles members.

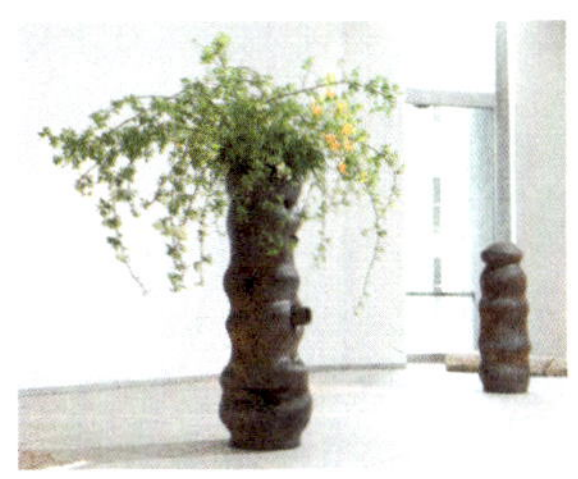

Hiroshi Teshigahara, Echizen ceramic ware, 1980, installation view, *Hengen—from Hiroshi to Akane*, Tokyo, April 2021.

The raw material aspect of Adam Silverman's vessels would have been familiar to Los Angeles ikebana senseis through their knowledge of stoneware objects originating from the six historic kilns of Japan. The founding headmaster Sofu established the importance of using contemporary containers and created ikebana works featuring ceramics by well-known artists on numerous occasions. Sofu's arrangements in stoneware pieces by Isamu Noguchi are especially well documented. Noguchi began experimenting with earthenware in the 1930s, exploring and abstracting primitive forms of ancient Japanese clay sculptures. Between 1950 and 1952, Noguchi's sculptural stoneware celebrated the various types of earth found in the historic kiln locations of Japan, including Ibaraki, Seto, Shigaraki, Karatsu, and Bizen. The third headmaster of Sogetsu, Hiroshi Teshigahara, established his own kiln in Echizen, another historic kiln site, where he created a huge body of work—including dozens of evocative biomorphic forms made from local dark brown clay. The kiln is still in use by Hiroshi's daughter Akane, who is the fourth head of the school. Adam's earthen pots and wood-ash glazes evoke pottery from these regions, like Shigaraki, known for its crackled finish and random drips resulting organically from the firing process.

Another important aspect of the Sogetsu school is the relationship of ikebana to art. One of the school's founding principles is that ikebana itself is a contemporary art form, so interaction and collaboration with artists in other disciplines is an important part of the school's history, especially since the 1950s. Promoted in the US and Europe by the art critic Michel Tapié, known for coining the term Art Informel to identify a new postwar international movement, the work of Sogetsu's founder, Sofu Teshigahara, was included in major exhibitions in New York, Turin, Venice,

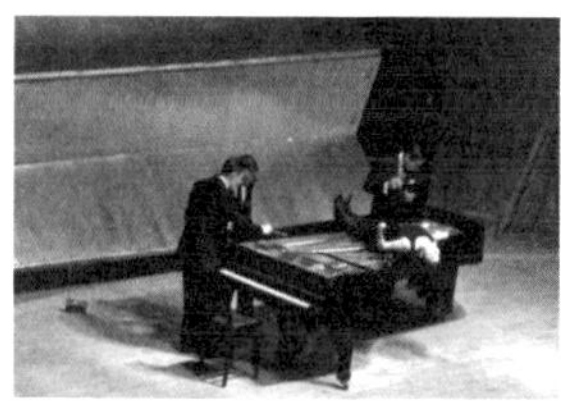

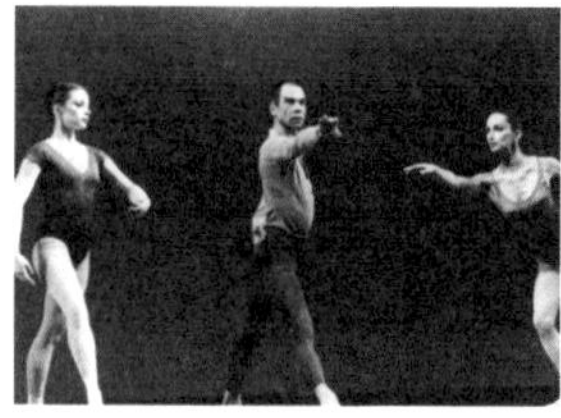

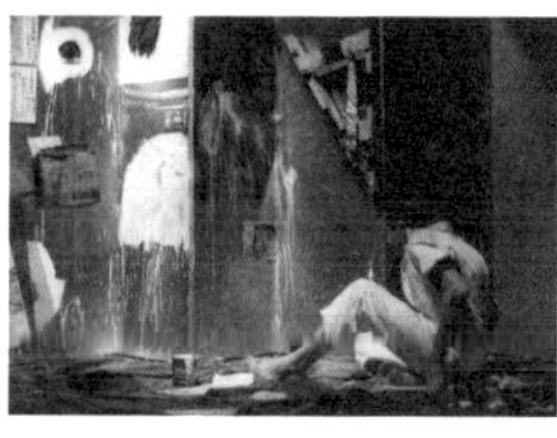

Top: From left, John Cage, David Tudor, Yoko Ono, and Toshiro Mayuzumi, 1962.

Center: Merce Cunningham Dance Company, November 1964.

Bottom: Robert Rauschenberg creating *Gold Standard* (1964) during *Twenty Questions to Bob Rauschenberg* performance, Sogetsu Art Center, Tokyo, November 28, 1964.

Amsterdam, and Paris, alongside such artists as Jean Dubuffet, Clare Falkenstein, Lucio Fontana, Georges Mathieu, and Antoni Tapies. During a visit to Paris in the early 1950s, Sofu formed a friendship with artist Sam Francis, who he later invited to Japan. Upon arrival in Tokyo, Sofu commissioned a large mural painting by Francis, that held an honored position in the auditorium of the new Sogetsu headquarters built in 1957. The building and its Sogetsu Art Center became a locus for the contemporary arts in Tokyo in the 1960s, hosting lectures, dance and music performances, and film screenings. The various disciplines were hosted by distinct entities at the center under names like the Sogetsu Culture Club, Sogetsu Music Inn, the Modern Jazz Circle, and the Sogetsu Cinematheque, directed by Sofu's son Hiroshi, an artist and filmmaker at the time. Both Japanese and Western avant-garde artists were well represented here, including now world-renowned figures Toshi Ichiyanagi, Yoko Ono, Nam Jun Paik, the Gutai group, John Cage, David Tudor, and Merce Cunningham. The youthful Robert Rauschenberg, accompanying the Merce Cunningham Dance Company in 1964 as stage and costume designer, famously created his first combine, *Gold Standard,* on stage at the Sogetsu Art Center on a gold-leafed Japanese screen provided by Sofu. The center flourished until the early 1970s.

Interdisciplinary collaborations are less frequent but still noteworthy at the Sogetsu Los Angeles chapter. In recent years, Kaz Kitajima, a local master sensei, provided ikebana works for *KESHIKI: The Landscape Within,* the 2019 exhibition of regional ceramics at Japan House, the Los Angeles outpost of the Japanese Ministry of Foreign Affairs. In 2003, another high-ranking sensei, Haruko Takeichi, collaborated with world-renowned artist Sharon Lockhart on the

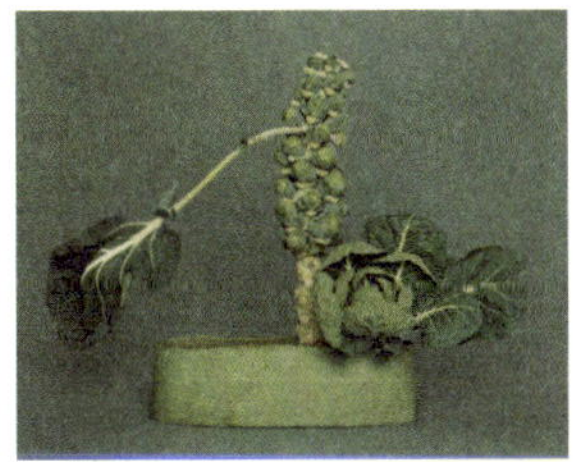

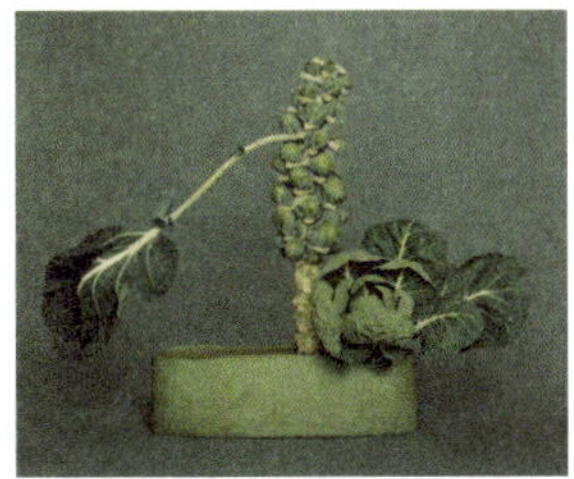

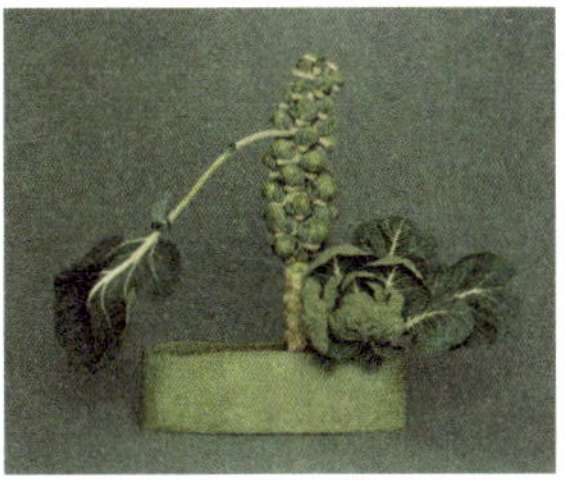

Sharon Lockhart, *NÕ-no Ikebana, arranged by Haruko Takeichi, December 1, 2002 (December 2–3)*, 2003. Three chromogenic prints, each 22.5 × 28 in.

serial work—*No-no Ikebana,* capturing the gradual wilting of an ikebana arrangement. Several senior branch members took part in *Living Flowers: Ikebana and Contemporary Art,* the seminal 2003 exhibition conceived by the late senior adjunct curator—Karin Higa—at the Japanese American National Museum. The show juxtaposed live ikebana arrangements with contemporary artworks relating to the floral art by international artists like Robert Mapplethorpe, Yukio Nakagawa, Isamu Noguchi, Gabriel Orozco, and Anna Sew Hoy.

The collaboration with Adam Silverman was an equally momentous occasion. Breaking the two-year isolation of the pandemic with such an extravagant display of ikebana and ceramics was a powerful experience for participants and viewers alike. Aligning with the concept of "common ground," the exhibition acknowledged the contributions of one immigrant minority community to the larger, inclusive view of American culture. The spectacle, spreading across the vast hall of the Japanese American Cultural and Community Center, recalled historic celebratory ikebana displays in ancient Kyoto and Edo, and marked the highest attendance for a Sogetsu Los Angeles event in recent times.

AKANE TESHIGAHARA

ON COMMON GROUND + SOGETSU LA

AKANE TESHIGAHARA
HEADMASTER,
SOGETSU JAPAN

INTERVIEWED BY
AYA MUTO

Sogetsu is known for its long history of collaboration with contemporary artists from various fields. Please share with us your view of this aspect of Sogetsu history. Why does Sogetsu encourage it? Why is it important? And does it continue to be an important aspect of Sogetsu's present?

My father's [former *iemoto*, or headmaster, Hiroshi Teshigahara] founding of the Sogetsu Art Center was historically significant and facilitated various collaboration projects at Sogetsu Hall in Tokyo during the 1960s. Artists and performers from a wide array of fields came together to work with Sogetsu and inspired one another, resulting in several important projects. Many artists went on to establish themselves as masters of their own art. Whether it is a filmmaker or a graphic designer, when I have an opportunity to interact with the contemporary Japanese greats, it is not unusual to hear how they used to frequent Sogetsu Hall back in the day. Considering how many years have passed, such connections ... are deeply valuable to us. We strive not only to master one field but to stay curious and be open to interaction; by stimulating each other we will be able to grow further and reach new territory. My father was an especially avid advocate for that attitude. There are definite philosophical links to the Sogetsu that I lead today; there is a particular environment that all Sogetsu members strive for.

Sogetsu *[the school's quarterly magazine] shares the collaborations and conversations between you and*

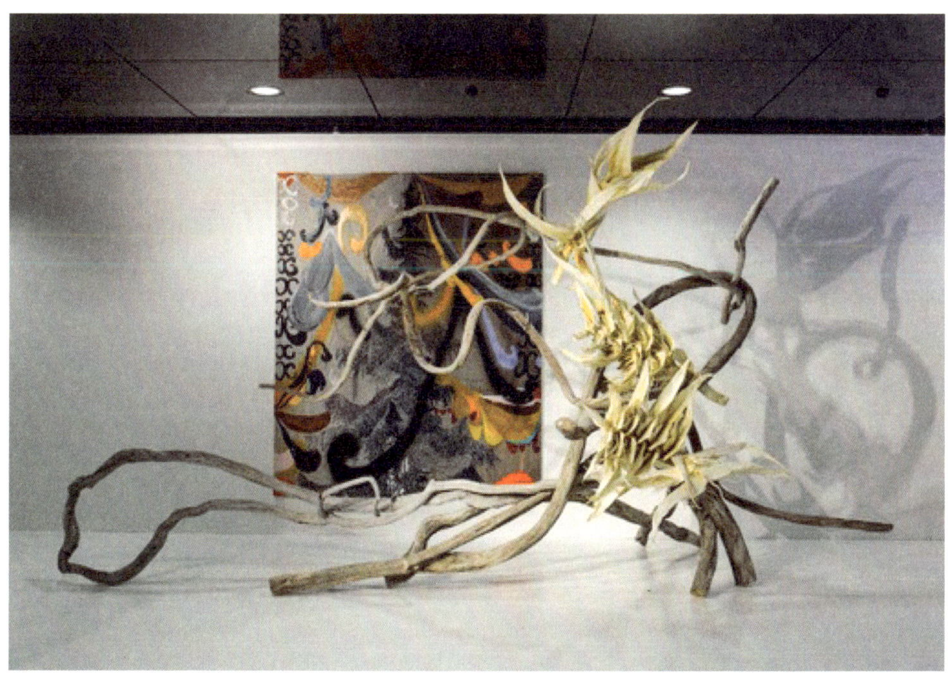

Installation view, *HANA SO*, 2017, Tokyo.

artists from different fields. When you embark on these collaborative projects, do you value the conversations around process as much as the final result?

In order to meet people in different fields, one must seek them out. We often stay focused on our own worlds, but any creative person can push the boundary by encountering something outside of one's comfort zone. There are many insights in such interactions. The more I grow, the more I aim to stay curious and meet all sorts of people in creative fields. Such experiences will keep us inspired.

At Sogetsu School in Japan, do you encourage individual artists or branch masters to collaborate with others?

Yes, and it has been that way from the time when my father was the headmaster. I have continued in that tradition too. The Sogetsu members who honor that history—I feel that they are already executing such projects. They have their own unique environments around them, which naturally leads to collaboration. Whenever I have a chance to see them work I'm often happily envious of their relationships. My environment is naturally different from another's, and you don't need to involve masters for all projects. By staying inquisitive, you allow an expression of creativity beyond ikebana—say with music or with moving images. I'm delighted to see that the Sogetsu members are proactively collaborating without being taught to do so.

What are some memorable collaborations with artists?

At Sogetsu, we have a decennial festival called Soryusai to commemorate the school's founding. The eightieth anniversary celebration, in 2007, was my first attempt at taking the stage as the new headmaster after the passing of my father. Having Ryōgoku Kokugikan, the national sports hall where Sumo tournaments are held, as the venue—with four stages—posed a challenge. I eventually decided to showcase the four seasons—using plants and collaborating with other creatives. That was when I met Kaiji Moriyama, a contemporary dancer who occupies his own world with a sensitive yet dynamic style. He produced one of the stages using dancers (including himself), percussion, and gospel music. I was especially intent on all elements, including the ikebana, meshing and inspiring each other. The flowers needed to embody equal energy and expression as the dance and the music they were sharing the stage with. It was a captivating and interesting project charged with intensity. Kaiji and I have worked together on different occasions ever since.

The scale and movement of an ikebana arrangement seems equally dynamic.

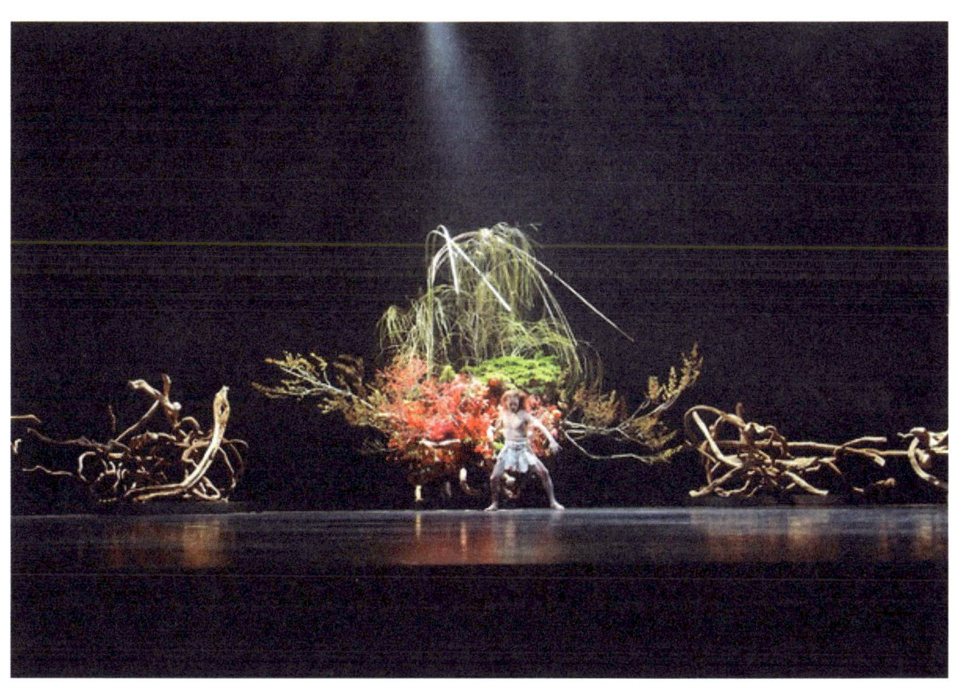

Dancer Kaiji Moriyama in front of Akane Teshigahara's set design for Act II: Demon Flowers of *Breath of Sound.*

It was really an interesting attempt to make Kaiji's energy work with my flowers. It was not soft nor was it merely beautiful. I believe in the strength, fright, and vigor that ikebana can embody. It might not be what people imagine at first, but through such collaboration, if I could show how intense ikebana expressions can be, I would be delighted.

There was a collaboration with calligrapher Koji Kakinuma published in Sogetsu, *and Koji was expressing how he was stunned to see you folding a leaf. Seeing the finished piece, one can imagine a snapping sound when you made that arrangement decision.*

Those arrangements were made in front of Koji, which made me realize unless you live in the ikebana world, it is not every day that you see someone work with flowers. That large leaf I folded to create an angle did make a noise, but we are used to them. That *snap!* seemed shocking

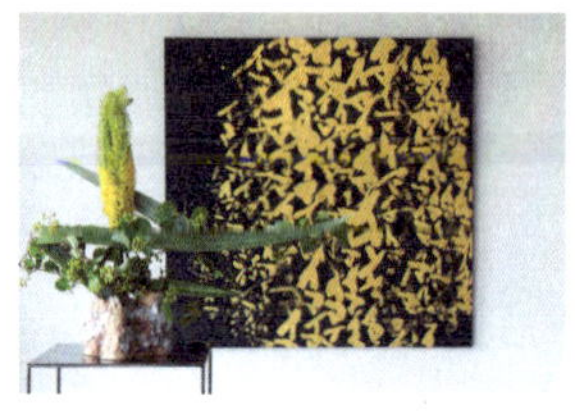

A folded-leaf arrangement made for a collaboration with calligrapher Koji Kakinuma.

to Koji—I remember him repeating "Wow!" I was happy that what he saw and experienced seemed fresh to him. Ikebana calls for spontaneous decision-making and these two arrangements were made on the spot without any preconceived ideas. I definitely felt his stare while I was working [laughs]. I owe it to his intense observation that I created with a certain speed evocative of making momentous decisions. That gave the pieces intensity, an element that might not have existed in an arrangement made with an abundance of time. Collaboration is interesting like that.

Please talk about HANA SO.

HANA SO was my solo exhibition that took place at the Sogetsu Kaikan [headquarters] in Tokyo, in 2017 to commemorate our ninetieth anniversary. As you enter Sogetsu Hall, the stone garden (titled *Heaven*) by Isamu Noguchi greets you, and I made ikebana installations there for this show. In the other areas of Sogetsu Kaikan, such as the lounge area and the traditional Japanese rooms, I have collaborated with six different artists. In our curriculum we talk about "complementing an artwork," and I wanted to showcase that theme through my collaborative arrangements. Paintings, sculptures, objects made with different mediums... working with all these different practices was truly interesting. It was an honor for me to make flower arrangements as if to interact with each piece and its own presence like in museum showcases. The playful element I was able to experience was the most interesting. In order to complement each artist's, I definitely was conscious about my ikebana being in harmonious coexistence with each art piece.

How would you describe the relationship between the arrangement and its vessel? Would you consider ceramics, compared with vessels made from other materials, as an important element of ikebana arrangement?

Once a year, I like to spend time at the Sogetsu ceramic kiln and make my own pieces. I also visit a glass craftsman's shop to make glass vessels with their assistance. At Sogetsu, we teach that one can make one's own vessel as part of the process of creating an arrangement. Of course, to pick out an exciting vessel made by an artisan or an artist and to make an arrangement interacting with what it has to offer is also a fun way to approach ikebana. If you use your own vessel, that definitely brings another layer of experience to the arrangement. For us, vessels are not just functional but another element of expression to apply toward the final piece. Ceramics, glass, lacquerware, or iron works: we regard them as an important expression that happen to function as vessels too. That might be a very Sogetsu point of view. Ceramic vessels are special because your hands can make them from scratch. You knead the clay (I work with artisans who assist me in this) and what your hand forms becomes the piece eventually. With glass works, I am more dependent on the glass craftsman, and interaction with that medium is less direct. The fundamental involvement ceramic work allows brings out a whole different level of intimacy to the vessel. Earth becomes clay—and your hand can flatten it, coil it up, and form any shape that you desire. Creative decisions can get a head start here. For those of us working with flowers, ceramics are an attractive medium that allows us to explore the possibilities of arrangements, thinking of the relationship to the flower forms and functionality to hold water. That flexibility allows our expression to flourish. I believe that there is a deep connection between ikebana and ceramics.

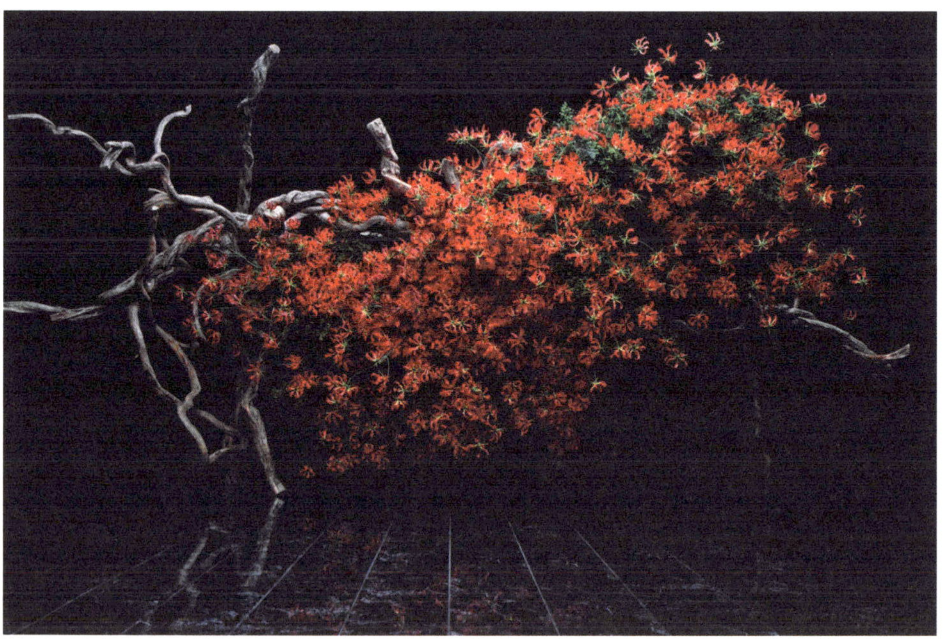

Akane Teshigahara, *Red Flowers* (2006). The twenty-two-foot-wide sculpture is composed of 1000 glory lilies.

Do you have a particular vessel choice you like to create your work with?

I always cherish the encounter even when I am working with flowers. I tend not to premeditate and remain open to happenstance. There's no right or wrong in this because there are many artists who prefer to pre-plan everything and execute beautifully. I just happen to be on the opposite end of the spectrum. I strongly believe in expressing what has come to me in the moment. Especially with ceramics, I am at ease because I'm an amateur at this medium, which grants me a degree of freedom. I would not hesitate to change what I'm doing if it no longer seems interesting, and that attitude definitely helps me truly have fun with it. This was true with my father too, but of course there are basic skills in ceramics that we must learn in the beginning. However, at quite an early stage, ceramics allows us to work freely. That freedom makes this medium very attractive.

For someone like me, if there are too many rules to follow, I may not continue doing it. The infinite possibility that ceramics embodies is one of the reasons I find this medium interesting.

Historically, are ikebana artists known to collect vessels? If you could also elaborate on the cultural significance of vessels to the Sogetsu School and talk about Sogetsu's special collection of ceramics.

Especially at Sogetsu, as we teach that vessels are part of one's expression, I believe many have an eye for vessels as valuable objects. I suspect that not many people would always want to work with the same vessel. Many are keen to follow ceramic artists' exhibitions and obtain pieces that they are drawn to, and even if you cannot own everything you are attracted to, you can share among friends who have different vessels. My grandfather Sofu [Teshigahara, founder of the Sogetsu School] had an extensive collection of vessels—some of them from artists like Picasso, Isamu Noguchi, and Rosanjin—which we maintain as Sogetsu's special collection today. That part of Sogetsu's history is a luxury that benefits all of us. If one were to be offered an opportunity to work with such vessels, it would be nerve wracking, but also a delight. People who truly enjoy working with flowers would definitely have a philosophy about the vessels they chose. At the Sogetsu School, there are no rules for vessels, so I believe many would have their own collection reflecting their taste and aesthetics.

Would Sogetsu's special collection of vessels ever be exhibited to the public?

Unfortunately, we cannot always use these valuable vessels for arrangements, but we once had a showcase called *Ikebana in Collected Containers.* Notable vessels from the collection were made available to 220 members, and that turned into quite a competition! Occasionally, I would bring out a piece from the Sogetsu collection as part of a lecture—or for an exhibition, for people to experience it in that way. Just the fact that such historical collections exist within the school stimulates creativity and I am aware that we are lucky to be in proximity to them. On the other hand, my father was an avid seeker of up-and-coming artists, inviting them to exhibit at Sogetsu Kaikan, and even made an open call to the public to discover new talent. For me it doesn't have to be an established master's work, but I would collect things that instinctually impressed me, or drew me in.

Your collection is an ongoing endeavor—which we get to look forward to. I am sure as a ceramic artist Adam would one day like for you to work with his pieces.

Oh yes, for sure. His vessels at this exhibition had such unique expressions that it made me want to work with them. Also, the diversity of clay among the fifty-six states and territories was impressive. Sogetsu's ceramic studio is in Fukui prefecture, using the clay that is called echizen. The texture and color of clay changes even within that small area. To work with the vast region that makes up the US, and specific clays from fifty-six different locales, that effort itself is breathtaking.

One of the things that left an impression on me, through talking to Ravi GuneWardena [former Sogetsu Los Angeles director] and other Sogetsu Los Angeles members, was the ephemeral aspect of the arrangement. I was told that this installation was on view longer than exhibitions usually are, so some artists might come and rearrange during the three weeks, and Ravi specifically mentioned his intention to show the decay of the leaf as part of his piece. The transient element that is plant matter, and vessels as something solid and unchanging—that interaction/conversation was interesting too.

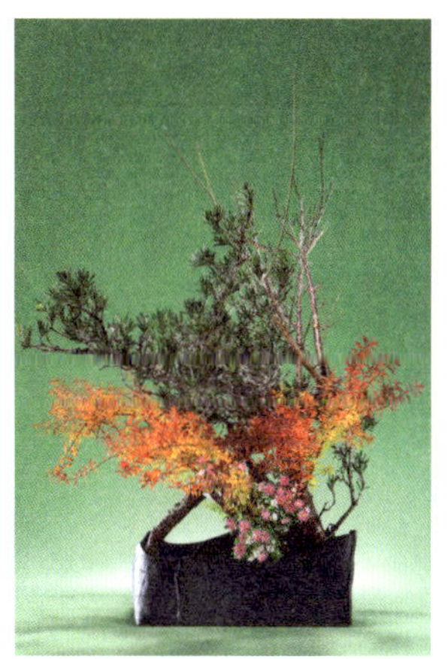

Akane Teshigahara, *Flowers of the season: November.* Arrangement includes Thunberg spirea, Japanese apricot, Japanese podocarp, and China aster, in a vase by Teshigahara.

Plants exemplify life. If the exhibition is up for a while, one might need to seek a way to constantly maintain the utmost beauty the arrangement is able to achieve. Or, like Ravi, to showcase the ephemeral and to observe the decaying of the leaves—that is an expression also. These transitions are expressions that were at play throughout the exhibition—the way the leaf curls, the way the color changes. To notice those elements and passing of time is the interesting aspect of working with living things.

POTTERY IS VITAL

TONY MARSH

Pottery has been a part of human civilization throughout history, evolving relative to available materials, crafting skills, technology, and functional and cultural needs. It carries forward collective cultural value, identity, and commemoration.

Pots are our earliest negotiations with earth science and fire, our first alchemy, a powerful intersection of nature and culture. Forever encoded in them are the DNA of the earth, the human creativity that made them, and the people who went on to use them. Pots are foundational devices of ritual and ceremony, they carry and deliver messages, they hold and project forward cultural memory.

Pottery is vital. Enter Adam Silverman and his *Common Ground* project.

Among the many worthy tasks of this group of fifty-six pottery vessels is to participate in staging ceremony and ritual. Silverman's base forms are classical in some ways but their handling is expressionist and naturalist in others. Silverman's pottery offers strong, subtle forms that embody anthropomorphic qualities and show signs of an inner life. Interestingly, looked at simply by shape, it is difficult to clearly assign a singular cultural identity. They are perhaps more pancultural than unicultural. It is a vessel form that we all know and are very comfortable with, they exemplify

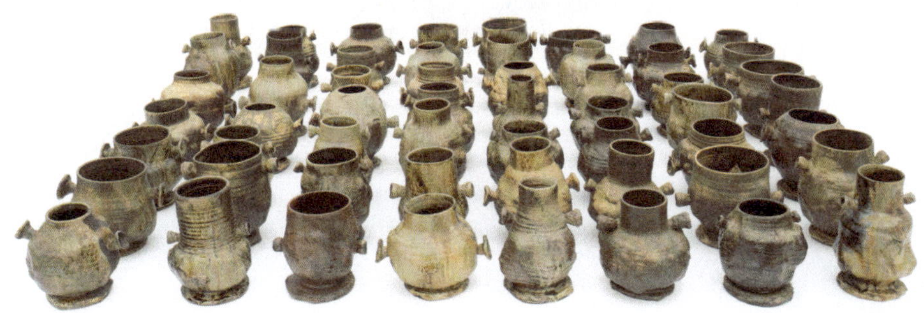

Adam Silverman, *Common Ground,* 2022.

what pots are. It is easier to detect a clear cultural influence in the surface treatment as one coming from the East. The pots have been ash-glazed—a reference to Japanese wood-fired pottery, offering subtle, variable effects and a cultural nod to Japanese aesthetics.

In the Sogetsu ikebana iteration of *Common Ground*, it is the ceramic vessel made by a single potter, with minor shifts in balance and scale that creates a stable constant in the project. With each of the fifty-six vessels installed by a different practitioner of Sogetsu ikebana, it is arrangements of living plant material that provide the dynamic variables. Adam Silverman's pieces in this project are cultural messengers, ambassadors of good will that act as objects of a particular natural beauty, carriers of the raw material of the land from where they came and the essence of the elements of a carefully considered communal project designed to heal. In that, Silverman's pottery behaves in both a cultural and natural context, projecting beauty and social messaging.

COMMON GROUND MATERIALS

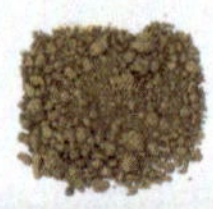

ALABAMA
Natalie Chanin,
Florence

Clay: From my home garden.

Wood ash: From the fireplace at my granddaughter's home. Partially a fire we shared one evening during the pandemic with family.

Water: From my home kitchen.

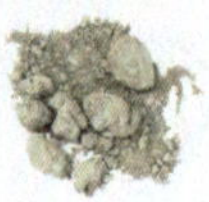

ALASKA
Kord Chistianson,
Sitka

Clay: Geologically, the Sitka area is relatively new because the area was covered by about two miles of glacial ice approximately 12,500 years ago. After the ice melted, the reduction of weight has caused the ground to (slowly) rebound, thus this area of Alaska is one of the few areas of the world where sea levels are falling. As a result, the availability of the clay is limited and generally poor quality (receding glacial rock mixed with volcanic ash). Ash from Mt. Edgecumbe, an extinct (last eruption 8,000–10,000 years ago) volcano located about twelve miles from Sitka has mixed with glacial silt to form clay. No local pottery is made from it (to my knowledge) so I assume it is of poor quality.

Wood ash: The wood enclosed is from this vintage World War II army tugboat that was wrecked on our family island homestead in 1970 after being grounded on a reef near Sitka. Time, decay, and marine life have taken their toll as she returns to this earth.

Water: Sitka has an annual rainfall of approximately eighty-five inches per year. Living on a twenty-six acre island we capture rainwater for drinking water. The water enclosed is—rainwater—recovered from the sky.

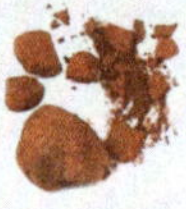

AMERICAN SAMOA
Reggie Meredith
Fitiao,
Leone Village Pago
Pago

Clay: Called "Eleele" from the stream in Malota. We use this to make our tapa cloth paintings called *siapo*.

Wood ash: From Leone. We make an—*umu*—for our way of cooking outdoors using all natural materials: woods, coconut shells, leaves, and river rocks.

Water: A combination of collected water drops from the leaves of taro, papaya, passionfruit, red ginger, bird of paradise, and a rain catchall.

ARIZONA
Steve Krafft,
Phoenix

Wood ash: Mesquite and applewood from the Hillside Spot Cafe's wood-fire oven.

Water: Tap water.

Peter Held,
Chandler

Clay: Mission clay from a clay mine in Prescott.

Wood ash: Don Reitz ranch, Clarkdale, AZ. 1 bag walnut, 1 bag cottonwood and pine mix.

Water: ⅓ rainwater, ⅔ tap.

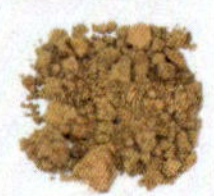

ARKANSAS
Linda Lopez,
Fayetteville and
West Fork

Clay: Bryce Brisco Pottery West Fork, Arkansas. Clay from driveway.

Wood ash: Our fireplace, Wedington Woods, Fayetteville. Wood sourced from Wedington Woods.

Water: Skull Creek, Fayetteville.

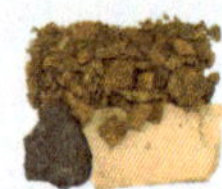

CALIFORNIA
Mariah Nielson,
Inverness

Wood ash: The fireplace in the JB Blunk house, Inverness.

Water: JB Blunk's studio sink, Inverness.

Adam Silverman and
Charlotte Silverman,
Malibu

Clay: Side of the road in the canyons.

Wood ash: Brush and forest fire, side of road.

Water: Pacific Ocean.

Tony Marsh,
San Pedro

Clay: San Pedro backyard.

Water: Cistern rainwater.

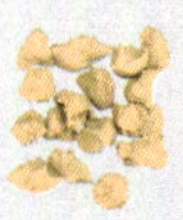

COLORADO
Darrin Alfred,
Denver

Wood ash: Outdoor fire pit.

Water: Cherry Creek.

Del Harrow,
Fort Collins

Clay: From a construction site in downtown. Much of the soil here has a high clay content and once you go down a few feet there are bands of pretty pure clay. It's mostly a red and brown color.

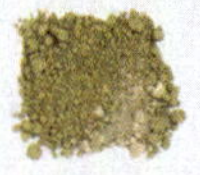

CONNECTICUT
Ana Rosa Aboitiz (Dinky),
Sharon

Clay: Nearby dirt road—Loper Road.

Wood ash: Taken from my fireplace—wood is local oak and ash.

Water: From our well.

Tyler Morgan,
Watertown

Clay: Brick making facility, South Windsor.

Wood ash: My fireplace.

Water: Smith pond.

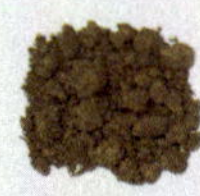

DELAWARE
Taylor Patterson,
Rockland

Clay: Brandywine Creek State Park.

Wood ash: Burn pile (most recent firing in October).

Water: Local creek.

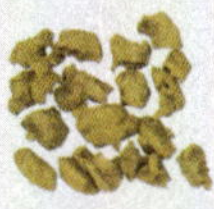

FLORIDA
Herrick H. Smith,
St. Augustine

Clay: Roadcut.

Wood ash: Ash chamber (oak and citrus).

Water: Rain collection.

The oldest documented Native American pottery found here is from approximately 3000 BCE. This is conceivably some of the same, or similar clay, as clay beds are somewhat rare here.

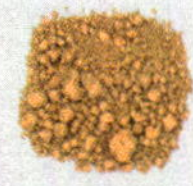

GEORGIA
Andrea Clark,
Warrenton

Clay: Turned-over earth from road digging on old farmland.

Wood ash: Georgia pine.

Water: Local spring.

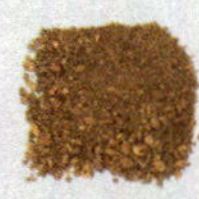

GUAM
Marinna Julian,
Chalan Pago

Clay: Nimitz Hill.

Wood ash: Nimitz Hill.

Water: Tumon Bay.

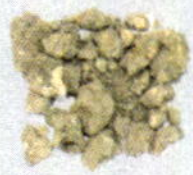

HAWAI'I
Morgan Garcia and Darcy Bartoletti,
Kapa'a, Kaua'i

Clay: Salt Pond beach.

Wood ash: Kealia beach Kapa'a tradition to burn your Christmas tree on New Year's Eve. This is the ash from our tree.

Water: Saltwater from Keali.

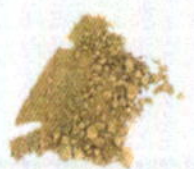

IDAHO
Jonathan Sadler,
Boise

Clay: Backyard, about ten inches deep.

Wood ash: Our fireplace.

Water: Our well

I was burying a hen who we have had for years. She must have been at least twelve years old, when we discovered the clay.

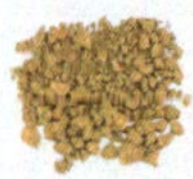

ILLINOIS
John W. Smith,
Enfield

Clay: Aunt's house.

Wood ash: Cousin's house.

Water: Mother's house.

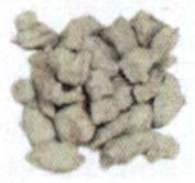

INDIANA
Rowland Ricketts,
Bloomington

Clay: Clay City.

Wood ash: Burned at home.

Water: Rainwater collected for dye studio.

The ash and water are materials I use in my own studio. The clay comes from a local potter named Walt Schmidt who gets his clay from the aptly named town of Clay City.

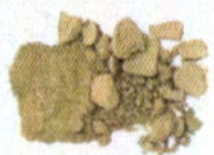

IOWA
Brant Weiland,
Iowa City

Clay: Clear Creek River, Iowa City.

Wood ash: Wood kiln fire box.

Water: Iowa River.

The source of the water is from directly in front of the Stanley Art Museum and Iowa Fine Art campus. This river flooded part of the state (2008) and had a seismic effect on the town and program.

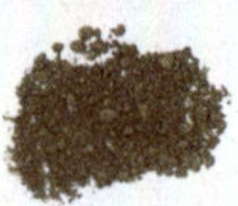

KANSAS
David Douglass,
Kansas City
(Prairie Village)

Clay: Backyard.

Wood ash: Wood ash was from a backyard tree.

Water: Tap.

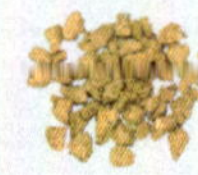

KENTUCKY
Peter Tate,
Stanford

Clay: Farm in Lincoln County.

Wood ash: Fireplace at home in Lexington.

Water: A spring on the farm in Lincoln County.

LOUISIANA
Helaine Moyse,
Baton Rouge

Clay: Alligator Bayou.

Wood ash: Live oak tree.

Water: Baton Rouge tap.

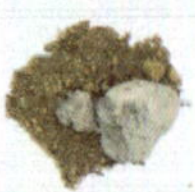

MAINE
Lareese Hall,
Waterville

Clay: Garden.

Wood ash: Fireplace.

Water: Snowfall.

Jeremy Frey,
Eddington

Clay: Penobscot River. The clay has been used by the Penobscot tribe for ages and was harvested near an ancient village site.

Wood ash: Eddington.

Water: Penobscot river.

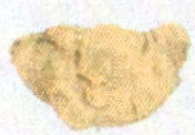

MARYLAND
Lisa Yanni,
Bethesda

Clay: Potomac riverbed.

Wood ash: Local trees chopped by my husband and father-in-law and burned in the in-laws wood stove.

Water: The pond in my backyard.

MASSACHUSETTS
Robbie Heidinger,
Westhampton

Clay: Mutt clay mixed with sand from the Dead Branch River in Chesterfield.

Wood ash: Western Massachusetts.

Water: Western Massachusetts well water.

The clay is my expression. The wood ash is a part of our life's cycle of stacking and heating, and the water is our liquid gold.

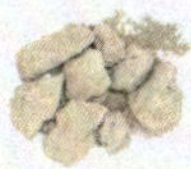

MICHIGAN
Jason S. Wesaw,
Bangor

Clay: Small inlet stream a few hundred yards from Lake Michigan, near Bridgman.

Wood ash: Backyard fire pit.

Water: Mkedé zibe (Black River, near Bangor).

I'm an artist and also Potawatomi, a small tribe that has remained in our ancestral homelands for thousands of years. My work as an artist is rooted in the land and reflective of my tribal culture.

The clay I harvested is used to make pieces I call—smudge bowls—or larger vessels to boil maple sap in the springtime. As a small Native American tribe, our continued, deep connection to this land is a major aspect of our identity. It teaches us. It nurtures us. It has sustained us for generations and will continue to do so, long after we are gone.

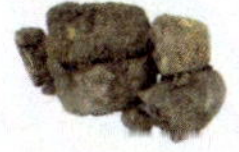

MINNESOTA
Lance Cyril Mountain,
Waconia

Clay: Woods in Waconia.

Wood ash: Woods in Waconia.

Water: Creek that runs from Lake Waconia to Burandt Lake.

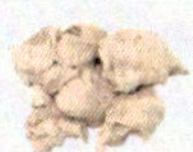

MISSISSIPPI
Peter Woods,
Mound Bayou

Clay: Peter's Pottery Mound Bayou.

Water: Mound Bayou.

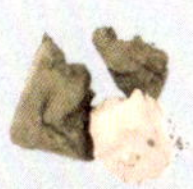

MISSOURI
Johnathan Stitelman,
University City

Clay: Craft Alliance Pottery Studio.

Wood ash: Seasoned oak from Fred Stiver's backyard fire pit.

Water: Missouri River—sourced tap water.

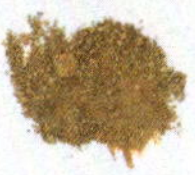

MONTANA
Raven Halfmoon,
Helena

Clay: Cliffside, ten miles outside Helena.

Wood ash: Wood-fired kiln. Cottonwood and cedar.

Water: Tap water.

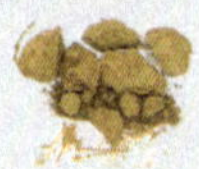

NEBRASKA
Peter Scherr,
Bellevue

Clay: There are six clays: Two from Bellevue, Lincoln, Endicott, Marquette, Nelson. It seems like most clays from this region (alluvial, sedimentary and loess) mature at about four to seven, and melt soon after. I've never seen a white clay, except out in Western Nebraska, where there are lots of bentonite type clays.

Wood ash: My backyard firepit and from my childhood house in Hastings.

Water: Rainwater collection.

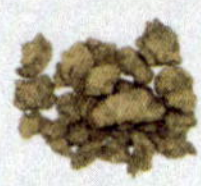

NEVADA
Jesse Combs,
Reno

Clay: A trail above the Truckee River across from Mayberry Park in West Reno.

Wood ash: Truckee River drift-wood, burned in my fireplace.

Water: Truckee River.

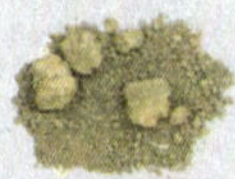

NEW HAMPSHIRE
Shana Brautigam,
Rindge

Clay: Durham, New Hampshire. Dug pond in close proximity to the Great Bay.

Wood ash: Mixed local hardwoods burned in home woodstove.

Water: Tap water from artesian well.

I dug the clay in the early years of my clay journey—probably around 2000). I have used it to make some low-fire pots, bricks, mixed it into glaze and slips, and used it in cob oven construction.

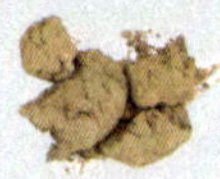

NEW JERSEY
The Hellenborg family,
Summit

Clay: Watchung Reservation.

Wood ash: Firepit in Watchung reservation.

Water: A creek in the reservation.

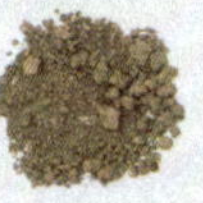

NEW MEXICO
Brian Paccione,
Las Trampas

Clay: From the holy ground in front of the church where many past Las Trampas are buried.

Wood ash: Annual Christmas bonfire outside the church.

Water: Rainwater collected from the roof of the church.

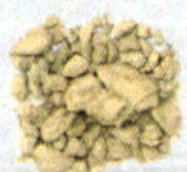

NEW YORK
Glenn Adamson,
Highland

Clay: Our backyard.

Wood ash: Wood from our yard burned in a soapstone stove.

Water: From our house well.

Marc Benda and family,
Shelter Island

Clay: Our garden.

Wood Ash: Our fireplace.

Water: Wades Beach.

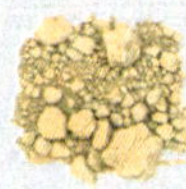

NORTH CAROLINA
Alex Matisse,
Asheville

Clay: First Broad River, Rutherford county, NC. Potter and friend Mike Ball brought me the clay.

Wood ash: The wood stove in our house in Asheville, with the trees being felled in Madison County.

Water: Tap water.

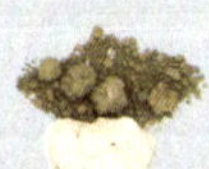

NORTH DAKOTA
Tama Smith,
Beach

Clay: A brickyard in Hettinger.

Wood ash: Theodore Roosevelt National Park campground.

Water: Little Missouri River.

Carrie Sapa,
Grand Forks

Clay: Grand Forks County.

Wood ash: Oak wood from Riverside Park.

Water: English Coulee.

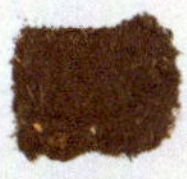

NORTH MARIANA ISLANDS
TJ Manglona,
Saipan

Clay: San Vicent, near Lao Lao Bay.

Wood ash: From a bbq in Kagmon, Saipan.

Water: Oleai Beach.

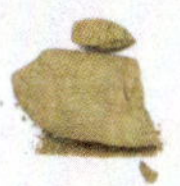

OHIO
Seth Nagelberg,
Shaker Heights

Clay: Orchard Hills Parks, Chesterland.

Wood ash: Fire pit at kiln site, Kirtland.

Water: Creek in Pepper Pike.

This was a collective project. Clay was provided by Alberto Veronica Lopez. Wood ash was provided by Seth Nagelberg. Water was provided by Misha Villanueua.

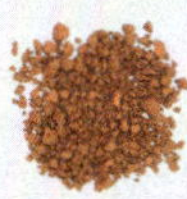

OKLAHOMA
Garrett Colton,
Oklahoma City

Clay: Clay was sourced from the ceramics studio manager at Oklahoma Contemporary.

Wood ash: My neighbor's fire pit.

Water: Local tap water.

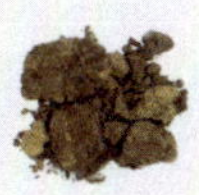

OREGON
Julie Weiss,
Portland

Clay: A friend's garden.

Wood ash: Fireplace ash.

Water: Sandy River.

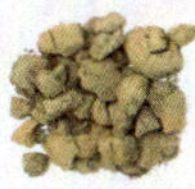

PENNSYLVANIA
Gregg Moore,
Glenside

Clay: A seam of clay that is exposed at the edge of a creek that runs through the Arcadia University campus.

Wood ash: Wood oven.

Water: The creek that exposed the clay.

All of the materials connect to a course I teach at Arcadia on the co-evolution of ceramics and cuisine. The clay was used to build the oven from which the ash is sourced. The water from the creek exposed the clay.

PUERTO RICO
Luis R. Beauchamp,
Maricao

Clay: Maricao River.

Wood ash: Cooking site at the river.

Water: Maricao River.

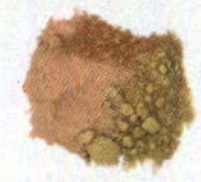

RHODE ISLAND
Adam Silverman,
Wakefield and Matunuck

Clay: Matunuck Town beach dunes.

Wood ash: Trees from Wakefield.

Water: Atlantic Ocean salt water and a well in Wakefield.

Bea Bestor and
Charlotte Silverman,
Block Island

Clay: Clay Head dunes.

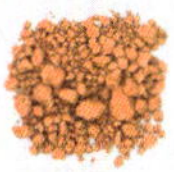

SOUTH CAROLINA
Spencer Bautista,
Greenwood

Clay: Collected from an area of undeveloped land next to my house.

Wood ash: Result of a firing experiment.

Water: Collected after a thunderstorm.

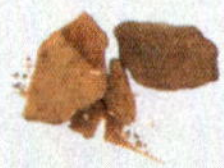

SOUTH DAKOTA
Michele Vento,
Custer County

Clay: Samples from French Creek River, Custer State Park land. The land where I live.

Wood ash: Found a Campfire near the French Creek trailhead in Custer State Park.

Water: French Creek, Custer State Park.

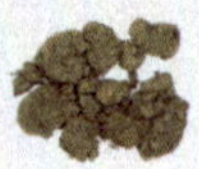

TENESSEE
Nico Aria and
Carter Little,
Nashville

Clay: Edwin Warner Park.

Wood Ash: Home fireplace.

Water: Edwin Warner Park Creek.

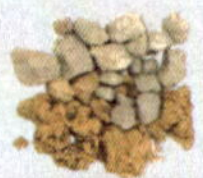

TEXAS
Jamey Garza,
Marfa

Clay: Clay scraped from the side of a five-foot-deep pit, West Heights neighborhood.

Wood ash: From the main smoker at Convenience West BBQ in Marfa. The oak wood that became the ash was from dead oak trees from the Fletcher ranch in Marfa. The Fletcher has been run for years by the Aufdengarten family.

Water: Tap water.

Adam Silverman,
Fort Worth

Clay: Kimbell Art Museum construction site.

Wood ash: Trees burned from the Kimbell site.

Water: Kimbell Art Museum fountain and Forth Worth Modern Art Museum fountain.

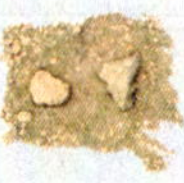

UTAH
Bree Phillips,
Salt Lake City

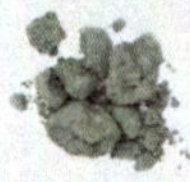

VERMONT
Nicole Antac,
Sharon

Clay: Small brook under a water bed near Quimby Mountain.

Wood ash: Local oak and maple from my woodstove.

Water: Our well.

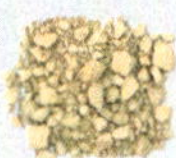

VIRGINA
Michelle Erickson,
Hampton

Clay: Site of 10,000 years of Indigenous settlement, Carter's Grove, Williamsburg.

Wood ash: Collected rush pine driftwood from Carter's Grove shoreline on the James River.

Water: James River.

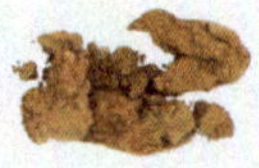

US VIRGIN ISLANDS
Tristin Armin
Edwald Mudarra,
Cruz Bay, St. John

Clay: Local salt pond.

Wood ash: Fireplace at home.

Water: Saltwater from the beach.

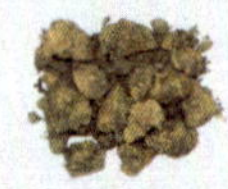

WASHINGTON
Julia Combs,
Josephine Lambert,
and Amy Lambert,
Seattle

Clay: Cliff face at Discovery Park.

Wood ash: Spruce and cotton-wood wood from a campground pit at Potholes State Park in eastern Washington.

Water: Salt water from Puget Sound.

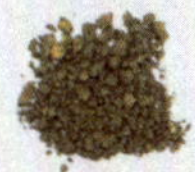

WASHINGTON DC
Jason Belle,
Washington DC

Clay: My backyard, Ledroit Park neighborhood.

Wood ash: Rock Creek Park.

Water: Reflecting Pool on the National Mall.

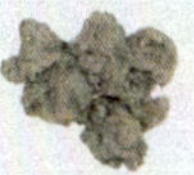

WYOMING
Kristina Loggia,
Wilson

Clay: Lower Slide Lake, Bridger National Forest.

Wood ash: Pine burned in our fireplace.

Water: Snake River.

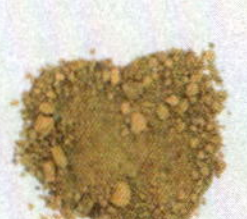

WEST VIRGINIA
Jeff Diehl,
Lockbridge

Clay: Back field.

Wood ash: Red oak in wood stove.

Water: Our pond.

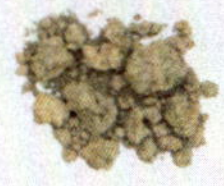

WISCONSIN
Michael Doyle Olson,
Madison

Clay: Construction site.

Wood Ash: Backyard fire pit.

Water: Lake Mendota.

IKEBANA MATERIALS

p.10
ALASKA
Haruko Takeichi

Sitka spruce (*Picea sitchensis*) and spiraea (*Spiraea cantoniensis*).

p.11
LOUISIANA
Amy Chuang

Dried yellow pampas grass (*Cortaderia selloana*), dried purple lagurus grass (*Lagurus ovatus*), red bud branches (*Cercis occidentalis*), craspedia (*Craspedia globosa*), and asparagus fern (*Asparagus setaceus*).

p.12
WEST VIRGINIA
Marilyn Drageset

Magnolia (*Magnolia × Soulangeana*), hydrangea (*Hydrangea macrophylla*), and acacia (*Acacia penninervis*).

p.13
FLORIDA
Atsuko Furuya

Orange blossom (*Citrus sinensis*), pygmy date palm (*Phoenix roebelenii*), and Bird of Paradise (*Strelitzia reginae*).

p.14
PENNSYLVANIA
Rie Strong

King protea (*Protea cynaroides*), banksia protea (*Banksia speciosa*), red dogwood branches (*Cornus sericea*), craspedia (*Craspedia globosa*), and eryngium (*Eryngium corniculatum*).

p.15
CALIFORNIA
Tony Shun

Protea empress (*Protea cynaroides*), Japanese maples (*Acer palmatums*), tree fern, (*Cyathea glauca*), and painted vine.

p.16
MARYLAND
Jina Choi Wakimoto

Quercus (*Quercus agrifolia*), Vitis (*painted*), wisteria (*Wisteria sinensis*), and chrysanthemum (*Chrysanthemum × morifolium*).

p.17
NEW JERSEY
Kazumi Geiger

Dried wood (*Cornus sericea*) and three different colors of oak leaves (*Quercus alba leaves*).

p.18
NEVADA
Davikja Wijesinghe

Palm bark fiber, craspedia (*Craspedia globosa*), narrow-leaf chalkstick (*Senecio vitalis*), tree houseleek (*Aeonium arboreum*), and gold leaf flakes.

p.19
VERMONT
Yumiko Inoue

Pine bark (*Pinus*), artichoke (*Cynara cardunculus*), and stone-flower (*Passiflora foetida*).

p.20
PUERTO RICO
Norma Mcdonough

Mexican fan palm (*Washingtonia robusta*), lobster claw (*Heliconia*), and hand-made plaster mask painted with acrylics.

p.21
MISSOURI
Naoko Zaima

Magnolia (*Magnolia grandiflora*).

p.22
COLORADO
Izumi Uemura

Cedrus atlantica, mimosa (*Mimosa pudica*), and lavender (*Lavandula*).

p.23
CONNECTICUT
Keiko Miyahara

Painted asparagus fern (*asparagus setaceus*) and statice (*Limonium sinuatum*).

p.24
MAINE
Lily Wu

Pine (*Pinus*) needles and cone, concrete tile, and copper wire.

p.25
UTAH
Rie Strong

Palm frond base (*Washingtonia robusta*), lobster claw heliconia (*Heliconia lennartiana*), parrot heliconia (*Heliconia psittacorum*), dried palm leaf (*Phoenix dactylifera*), pencil tree (*Euphorbia tirucalli*), and dried pampas grass (*Cortaderia selloana*).

p.26
ARKANSAS
Miko Usami

Cherry tree (*Prunus serrulata*), pine tree (*Pinus ponderosa*), and glass pieces.

p.27
SOUTH CAROLINA
Ravi GuneWardena

Sweet Bay Magnolia (*Magnolia viginiana*) and eastern redbud (*Cercis danadensis*).

p.28
MISSOURI
Naoko Zaima

Star pod (*Sterculia rogersii*), bittersweet branches (*Celastrus orbiculatus*), bottle tree bark (*Brachychiton rupestris bark*), chrysanthemum (*Chrysanthemum × morifolium*), leucadendron (*Leucadendron salignum*), eryngium (*Eryngium corniculatum*), globe amaranth (*Gomphrena globosa*), pandanus (*pandanus baptistii variegata*), song of India (*Dracaena reflexa*), and ruscus (*Ruscus hypoglossum*).

p.29
WISCONSIN
Michiko Amiya

Gladiolus (*Gladiolus grandifolia*), forsythia (*Forsythia × intermedia*), Gypsophila (*Gypsophila elegans*), cherry blossom (*Prunus serrulata*), ranunculus (*Ranunculus asiaticus*), and cheese boxes.

p.30
IOWA
Toko Okada

Oak (*Quercus agrifolia*), Siberian dogwood (*Cornus alba*), and statice (*Limonium sinuatum*).

p.31
MASSACHUSETTS
Norma Mcdonough

Pincushion proteas (*Leucospermum catherinae*), allium snake balls (*Allium obliquum*), flowering onion (*Allium schubertii*) dried and painted, and cattail (*Typha latifolia*) painted leaves.

p.32
ALABAMA
Mariko Ide

Camellia (*Camellia cultivar*) and longleaf pine (*Pinus palastrus*).

p.33
MICHIGAN
Michiyo Nakamura

Manzanita branches (*Arctostaphylos nevadensis*), moss (*Tillandsia usneoides*), painted asparagus (*Asparagus virgatus*), and rattan woven balls (*Calamus rotang*).

p.34
NORTH DAKOTA
Tory Lowitz

Plastic rain gutter foam, wire, and drywall screws

p.35
KANSAS
Kaz Kitajima

Pencil tree (*Euphorbia tirucalli*), and bark strips (*Brachychiton rupestris*).

p.36
INDIANA
Meg Shimizu

Painted palm leaf (*Washingtonia robusta*), peony (*Paeonia lactiflora*), eryngo (*Eryngium agavifolium*), and craspedia (*Craspedia globosa*).

p.37
OKLAHOMA
Kaz Kitajima

Raphiolepis pink lady (*Rhaphiolepis Indica*) and craspedia (*Craspedia globosa*).

p.38
TENNESSEE
Haruko Takeichi

Yellow poplar branches (*Liriodendron tulipifera*), cotton (*Gossypium herbaceum*), iris (*Iris latifolia*), anemone (*Anemone coronaria*), cast-iron plant (*Aspidistra elatior*) , and papier-mâché hoops.

p.39
GEORGIA
Miyako Arao

Dry cotton plant branch (*Gossypium herbaceum*), rose (*Rosa chinensis*), dried *Abelmoschus esculentus*, and ruscus (*Ruscus hypoglossum*).

p.40
VIRGINIA
Patricia Liu

Red dogwood sticks (*Cornus sericea*), epidendrum (*Epidendrum radicans*), blue anemone (*Anemone coronaria*), lacy tree philodendron (*Thaumatophyllum bipinnatifidum*).

p.41
WASHINGTON
Ayako Ariga

Manzanita (*Arctostaphylos manzanita*), Japanese andromeda (*Pieris japonica*), statice (*Limonium sinensis*), azalea (*Rhododendron variety*), dried blue hydrangea (*Calophyllum inophyllum*), and deer horn.

p.42
IDAHO
Chiyoko Chasin

Potatoes and potato leaves (*Solanum tuberosum*), craspedia (*Craspedia globosa*), and woven rattan (*Calamus rotang*).

p.43
KENTUCKY
Kumiko Nakao

Goldenrod (*Solidago altissima*) and moss (*Tillandsia usneoides*).

p.44
NEW MEXICO
Mayumi Hyodo

Aloe vera flowers (*Aloe barbadensis miller*), pencil cactus (*Euphorbia tirucalli*), aeonium arboreum, queen of the night stem (*Epiphyllum oxypetalum*), fishbone cactus (*Epiphyllum anguliger*), and grapevine (*Vitis vinifera*).

p.45
NEW HAMPSHIRE
Naomi Oki

White birch (*Betula papyrifera*), purple lilac (*Syringa vulgaris*), red box (*Eucalyptus polyanthemos*) and white paper.

p.46
ILLINOIS
Natsumi Laske

Bamboo (*Bambusa vulgaris*), sea holly (*Eryngium amethystinum*), golden wattle (*Acacia pycnantha*), carnation (*Dianthus*), and dried queen palm (*Syagrus romanzoffiana inflorescence*).

p.47
ARIZONA
Sandy Kitayama

Various succulents including climbing aloe (*Aloiampelos ciliaris*), hen-and-chicks (*Echeveria prolifica*), aloe vera (*Echeveria*).

p.48
OHIO
Keiko Miyahara

Sansevieria (*Dracaena trifasciata*) and scarlet carnation (*Dianthus caryophyllus*).

p.49
MONTANA
Yumiko Inoue

Dry eucalyptus (*Eucalyptus globulus*) stump, painted king protea (*Protea cynaroides*), and baby's breath (*Gypsophila elegans*).

p.50
TEXAS
Violet Shen

Delphinium (*Delphinium grandiflorum*), thistle (*Eryngium planum*), palm bark (*Washingtonia robusta*), and painted bird of paradise (*Strelitzia reginae*) leaves.

p.51
SOUTH DAKOTA
Toko Okada

Flowering cherry (*Prunus speciosa*), dried arctostaphylos manzanita, jade plant (*Crassula ovata*), lace flower (*Daucus carota*), and stone.

p.52
OREGON
Jessica Gardner

Western redbud (*Cercis Occidentalis*), calla lily (*Zantedeschia*), asparagus fern (*Asparagus setaceus*), and pine (*Pinus*).

p.53
US VIRGIN ISLANDS
Miyako Arao

White knobby starfish (*Protoreaster nodosus*), sea fan (*Gorgonia ventalina*), umbrella fern (*Sticherus cunninghamii*), Moth orchid (*Phalaenopsis*), painted yellow palm (*Dypsis lutescens*), and tropical fish ornaments.

p.54
NORTH CAROLINA
Christine Liao

Baby's breath (*Gypsophila*), asparagus fern (*Asparagus setaceus*), wire, bamboo strips (*Bambusa vulgaris*), and a 1903-Wright flyer model.

p.55
AMERICAN SAMOA
Ravi Gunewardena

Banana leaves and flower (*Musa ornata*), ginger (*Alpina purpurata*), palm leaves (*Pritchanrdia affinis*), and pampano plant (*Calathea lutea*).

p.56
NORTHERN MARIANA ISLANDS
Auralynn Nguyen

Western sword fern (*Polystichum munitum*), giant white bird of paradise (*Strelitzia nicolai*), pineapple flower (*Ananas comosus*), aspidistra (*Aspidistra eliator*), feverfew (*Tanacetum parthenium*), and bismarck palm (*Bismarckia nobilis*).

p.57
NEW YORK
LiHua Jenny Huang

Chicken wire, rose (*Rosa variety*), dogwood (*Cornus sericea*), and gold metal strip.

p.58
RHODE ISLAND
Tomokom Adams

Carnation (*Dianthus caryophyllus*), smoke tree (*Cotinus ovabatus*), maple tree (*Acer palmatum*), and grevillea (*Grevillea rosmarinifolia*).

p.59
GUAM
Susan Kang

Red ginger (*Alpinia purpurata*), cascade palm (*Chamaedorea cataractarum*), gravata (*Portea petropolitana*), and dried Alexandra palm (*Archontophoenix alexandrae*).

p.60
MINNESOTA
Dan Usami

Pine (*Pinus ponderosa*), palm (*Washington robusta, inflorescence*), red plastic tube, and automobile part.

p.61
WYOMING
Saeko Kujiraoka

Aeonium succulent (*Aeonium undulatum*), statice (*Limonium sinuatum*), and willow (*Salix matsudana*).

p.62
NEBRASKA
Shawna Schdmit

Mix of three prairie grasses and dried larkspur (*Delphinium elatum*).

p.63
DELAWARE
Alfonso Mendosa

Peach (*Prunus persica*), panicle hydrangea sepals (*Hydrangea paniculata*), bamboo (bambusa vulgaris), tangle fern (*Gleichenia dicarpa*), leatherleaf fern (*Rumohra adiantiformis*), money plant (*Lunaria annua*), and Eastern tiger swallowtail (*Papilio glaucus*).

p.64
WASHINGTON DC
Saeko Kujiraoka

Palm sheath (*Arecaceae*), ZZ plant (*Zamioculcas zamiifolia*), and statice (*Limonium pectinatum*).

p.65
HAWAII
Marilyn Drageset

Red heliconia (*Heliconia caribaea*), bird of paradise (*Strelitzia reginae*), pineapple (*Portea petropolitana*), pineapple (*Chrysanthemum morifolium*), willow branch (*Salix udensis Sekka*), and monstera leaves.

ACKNOWLEDGMENTS

Adam Silverman would like to acknowledge:

The land from which this project was born. It is a land that has welcomed and nurtured humanity, lived in harmony with its original occupants, and witnessed unspeakable violence and exploitation. I have attempted to treat the land used in *Common Ground* with the reverence and stewardship that it deserves; to honor everything that it may contain and represent for everyone who has, does, or will call this land home.

Sheikh Jassim Al-Thani for the conversation and idea that birthed the *Common Ground* project.

Ravi GuneWardena for being a great partner in every aspect of this collaboration, for your beautiful ikebana work and for your insightful text in this book.

Josh White for the gorgeous pictures that bring this project to life in print.

Sofu Akane Teshigahara, the fourth Iemoto of the Sogetsu Ikebana School in Tokyo. For your wisdom and generosity while speaking with Aya Muto about the history of Sogetsu, your work, and this collaboration within that important context.

Aya Muto for your insightful interview with Sofu Akane Teshighara and for your concise translation of it into English.

Tony Marsh for your expert and meaningful text on the empty *Common Ground* pots and placing them into context.

Erik Benjamins for the years of great *Common Ground* process photographs.

Each of the fifty-six Sogetsu artists who collaborated on this project, and who are individually credited elsewhere in the book.

The roughly seventy people who collected clay, wood ash, and water from across the country, who are individually credited elsewhere in this book, and the many people who connected me with those material collectors. It was a heroic group effort.

Hirokazu Kosaka and the staff of the Japanese American Cultural and Community Center in Los Angeles for hosting this collaborative exhibition.

The always brilliant and curious Scott Alves Barton, my friend and partner in *Common Ground*.

From my studio, essential support for this project was provided: John Reilly, Wally Wolodarsky, June Tate, Onni Estabrook, and James Burwick.

Steve Davis for his kazegama kiln design which has played an important role in the flavor of this project, and Mark Coppos for the actual kiln he handed down to me, a few years, and fifty firings ago.

Shannon Harvey, Adam Michaels, Ásta Þrastardóttir, and their team at IN-FO.CO for the elegant and intelligent design of this book, and for publishing it through Inventory Press, my gratitude is enormous.

The following people have offered deeply appreciated advice and wisdom throughout the making of *Common Ground*: Glenn Adamson, Scott Alves Barton, Marc Benda, Louise Bonnet, Lisa Mark, Lucas Michael, Michael Sherman, Lauren Taschen, Bobbye Tigerman, Lorraine Wild, and Erin Wright.

Marc Benda for the encouragement and support of this project and my work in general, and for orchestrating the meeting with Sheikha Mayassa Al-Thani and Sheikh Jassim Al-Thani that led to the birth of *Common Ground*.

Thank you Bea, Charlotte, Poppy, and Cosmo, who each contributed materials and much more to this project, and to my life.

And most importantly, thank you LB, without you there is nothing.

CONTRIBUTORS

RAVI GUNEWARDENA

Ravi GuneWardena is an ikebana teacher and former director of the Los Angeles branch of the Sogetsu School of Ikebana (2019–22). Originally from Sri Lanka, he studied architecture at California State Polytechnic University, Pomona, and art history in Florence, Italy. He has served on the Hollywood Public Art Advisory Panel for the Community Redevelopment Agency, Los Angeles. A principal at Escher GuneWardena Architecture, he has taught at Cal Poly Pomona, University of Oregon, and EPFL, the Swiss Federal Institute of Technology, Lausanne.

TONY MARSH

Tony Marsh is a sculptor and ceramist based in San Pedro, California. Marsh recently retired from full-time teaching at Cal State Long Beach where he chaired the ceramics program for twenty-five years and was the cofounder and first director of the Center for Contemporary Ceramics on campus. Marsh has exhibited in solo and group exhibitions since 1992. His work is in several prestigious international collections including the San Francisco Museum of Modern Art, the Metropolitan Museum of Art, Los Angeles County Museum of Art; Museum of Arts and Design; and the Museum of Fine Arts, Houston, among others.

AYA MUTO

Aya Muto is a freelance translator, writer, and photographer based in Los Angeles. Originally from Japan, she is a regular art, design, culture, and lifestyle contributor to *Casa Brutus*, *Brutus*, *Tsubasa*, and others.

ADAM SILVERMAN

Adam Silverman is a Los Angeles-based artist known for his experimental processes and resulting sculptural vessels. He is regarded as one of the most dynamic practitioners dedicated to ceramics today. Silverman received a BFA and a BArch from the Rhode Island School of Design He creates ambitious ceramic work using site-specific materials that engage their place of origin.

AKANE TESHIGAHARA

Akane Teshigahara became the fourth *iemoto* (headmaster) of the Sogetsu School of Ikebana in 2001. As the leader of Sogetsu—which respects free and liberated creation—she has pursued the potential of a new approach to ikebana suitable for an ever-changing modern world. She has actively engaged in collaborations with artists in different disciplines and has also presided over the Akane Junior Class, which aims to develop sensitivity and independence in young people through ikebana.

Adam Silverman:
Common Ground
is published by
Inventory Press
2305 Hyperion Ave
Los Angeles, CA 90027
inventorypress.com

Editor
Eugenia Bell

Design
IN-FO.CO (Adam Michaels,
Shannon Harvey,
Ásta Þrastardóttir)

Printed and bound in Belgium
by die Keure

ISBN: 978-1-941753-56-9
LCCN: 2023930953

All images courtesy the artist
unless otherwise noted.

Image Credits: pp. 2-5, 72, 76-91, 113: photos by Erik Benjamins; pp. 10-65, 66-71, 92-95: photos by Joshua White; p. 98: courtesy the Special Collection USDA National Agricultural Library; p. 100 (bottom): photo by Masaaki Sekiya © 2023 Robert Rauschenberg Foundation / Licensed by VAGA at Artists Rights Society (ARS), NY; p. 101: © Sharon Lockhart, courtesy the artist, Gladstone Gallery and neugerriemschneider, Berlin; p. 103: photo by Sekiya Kozo; courtesy Sogetsu Foundation; p. 105: courtesy Sogetsu Foundation; p. 106: photo by Kasai Arisa; courtesy Sogetsu Foundation; p. 108: courtesy Sogetsu Foundation; p. 111: photo by Ōzawa Chukyo; courtesy Sogetsu Foundation

Distributed by
ARTBOOK | D.A.P.
75 Broad St, Suite 630
New York, NY 10004
artbook.com